THREE CHURCHES IN RENEWAL

THREE CHURCHES IN RENEWAL

Lawrence O. Richards

ZONDERVAN PUBLISHING HOUSE
OF THE ZONDERVAN CORPORATION
GRAND RAPIDS, MICHIGAN 49506

Contents

1 « Show me

There's a tension in the air these days — a feeling that the time has come to stop living by habit, and to make basic decisions about where we are to go in our churches.

There's a flourishing of seminars: seminars on Church Management, on Kennedy Evangelism, on how to build Big Churches (held by pastors of the nation's dozen Superchurches) and on how to build renewal churches (conducted by such organizations as Step 2, led by Circle Church pastor David Mains). With all the competing views, with emphases on Church Growth and on Church Evaluation, there has come a certain skepticism. We've heard the challenge to the traditional church and the call for evangelical renewal for nearly a decade now. We've heard too the strident response of the Big Churches: Big is successful. Preach the Word, follow the strong pastor, and grow. For growth and only growth is the measure of church effectiveness.

What the renewal writers have to say sounds tremendously attractive. But what the Big Churches have accomplished seems impressive! And examination shows that the Big Church is built on the very principles the renewal movement is most critical of. Against all the persuasive argument and exposition of renewal, the example of the Big Church has stood unchallenged. And a very reasonable request has come from the friends and enemies of renewal alike: Give us examples of renewal. Show us what a biblical renewal can do, even as the Big Churches have shown us what happens when their concepts and principles are applied.

This has been a reasonable request, but a difficult one to

meet. In the first place, the rediscovery of the principles on which renewal suggests church life be structured is a relatively recent thing. The approach of the Big Church is hardly new: it has been used to build the giants that have been known for many decades in the South and North.

In the second place, the Big Church is a highly visible church. Its criterion of success is size, and size is a hard thing to disguise! But the renewal church does not measure effectiveness by size alone. In fact, the renewal church is more likely to foster a number of daughter churches rather than invest in gigantic and expensive physical plants. Thus the renewal church is not a visible church and not likely to be written up as one of "the Ten!"

A third reason for the difficulty in bringing forward examples of renewal churches is that the development of a healthy local body takes time. A number of years of *growing as a Body* under sensitive leadership is required before the signs of life and health postulated by renewal will be evident. (In each of the churches in this book, the growing time is almost ten years!)

Today there *are* a number of "renewal" churches maturing and demonstrating, in our country, the practical validity of the biblical principles renewal speakers and writers have emphasized. Today there are far more than the three described in this book; you'll read of some of them, like Salem, Oregon's Alliance Church, in new books soon to be published by a variety of publishers. Today we can definitely point to a number of churches around the country — and the number is growing — and say "Yes. Here is what we mean when we talk renewal. Here is an example of what it's like to build the local church on critical principles of church life presented in the Word of God."

Crucial principles

There are a number of concepts stressed by writers on church renewal. Several of the concepts are crucial — crucial because of their rooting in Scripture, and crucial because they are *necessary* dimensions of church life as this is understood from Scripture.

Unified Body. In evangelical renewal the individualism of the past has been balanced by the realization that the church is a community. Oneness is stressed in renewal: a oneness that is not rooted in conformity — in either minutiae of doctrine or behavior. Instead, the oneness sought is that expressed in Colossians: "Christ is all that matters for Christ lives in all" (3:11). It is not acceptance of a person because he is like us, but because God has already accepted Him for Christ's sake!

An example of this conflict in emphasis is seen in the stress in the church growth movement on homogeneous groupings. The theory is that to the extent there is cultural and socioeconomic likeness among members of a church, to that extent the church has greater potential for growth through appeal to that particular segment of society.

Chicago's Circle Church provides a countermodel: a model of the open church, which cuts across cultural and societal barriers. There old and young, black and white meet, retain their cultural identities, and seek to work out their oneness in Christ. Black co-pastor Clarence Hilliard is convinced that the church cannot truly be "the Church" unless rich and poor, white and black, men and women are actively accepted and the value of their differences to the oneness of the whole affirmed (cf. Eph. 2:11-22).

While few congregations have worked through the problems of seeking a truly open church, still it is fair to say that in renewal there is an emphasis on the body of Christ as well as the individual, and that an honest effort is made to reject conformity as the price of acceptance. Believers *are* one: demonstrating oneness to the world is a significant witness of the body.

Love life style. Renewal places great stress on Jesus' "new commandment." The many, many exhortations in the New Testament to love one another in practical ways loom large in renewal thinking.

One of the clearest marks of the kind of life style renewal proclaims is an intense awareness of loving and being loved by members of a local body.

This dimension of the church's life is particularly important in our age. We live in an era often characterized as "depersonalizing." Few individuals are valued for themselves. Even in churches, hierarchies of values have been established, based on performance in church activities. Regular attendance, service in teaching, committeeships, and more have all been used to classify and value individuals. The atmosphere of performance has caused persons to hide failures and pains, and has cut them off from intimacy.

Renewal writers, building on the biblical portrait of love within the body, emphasize the unconditionalness of Christian love. They stress the need to be open and honest with one another, to bear one another's burdens rather than criticize them, and to help each believer sense through the love of brothers and sisters the unconditional love of God.

Servant leadership. Cast against the strong, authoritarian leadership style of the Big Church, renewal promotes the servant role of pastoral leadership.

The contrasts between leadership styles are many. The authoritarian stresses the differences between his position and that of the people: the servant leader stresses being among them, as one of them, sharing a full humanity and having as intense a need of Jesus daily as any man. The authoritarian leader maintains the differences between his pastoral role and the role of laymen: the servant leader rejects the concept of "layman" and sees his task as building each believer's innate capacity for ministry. The authoritarian leader directs, and reserves the right to control as his alone: the servant leader sees decision as the function of Christ, and unity in sensing God's will as the mark of His direction.

While these contrasts do not necessarily fit (and are not meant to be charges against) leaders of the Big Churches, the less obtrusive place of the pastor is a significant emphasis of renewal. The redefinition of his role as a builder of others through interpersonal contacts is definitely a distinctive.

Ministering laity. Many of the Big Churches stress active involvement of laymen. Without hundreds visiting, witnessing, and canvassing for bus routes, the Big Church could not be built.

But this is not what the renewal writer has in mind when speaking of a ministering laity. Rather than task roles, renewal thinks of ministry in terms of gifts — gifts in operation as members of the body minister to each other in sharing and interaction. These gifts, which include teaching, helping, showing mercy, and *all things* which build up the believer in the body, are not actually "tasks." They are not viewed in the framework of jobs (such as Sunday school teacher, bus canvasser) at all! Rather, they are viewed in the context of the contributions each believer makes *as a person* when he interacts with others in the body around Jesus Christ as the Word.

This building-up ministry is not limited, of course, to believers with one another. Gifts enable believers to witness effectively to others, to share and show Christ's reality and sufficiency. But again, the ministry is not seen in the framework of the organized task, the "church job." It is seen in the witness of who the believer *is*, and in the overflow of a life that Jesus is filling with Himself.

Growth emphasis. In harmony with these tendencies, renewal does put emphasis on growth. But it is personal and bodily spiritual growth; it is maturity toward Christlikeness rather than organizational expansion.

This emphasis in personal growth and development is not at the *expense* of numerical growth. It is instead a reflection of the belief that mature believers *will* reproduce themselves. And it is based on the conviction that *discipleship* — not just the initial conversion — is the goal of evangelism.

Renewal proponents note that while we have consistently had the Big Church over the decades, our evangelism has never matched that of the early church! Within two generations a large percentage of the people in the ancient world had heard and responded to the gospel. In some areas believers threatened to become a majority, a condition Tertullian said encompassed all of coastal Africa in his day! The Big Church strategy has not proved capable of reaching and winning a majority in our society. Renewal evangelism, built on distinctively different concepts and principles, now claims not only the right but also the urgent necessity of testing its strategy!

Scripture/response. Like the Big Churches, evangelical renewal claims a deep commitment to the Word of God. Yet there are distinct emphases in approach to Scripture. Renewal proponents are less concerned with definitions of doctrine, more concerned with daily, obedient response to what God is saying to us in His Word.

The resistance to making doctrinal purity the test of acceptance should not be misunderstood as disinterest or denial of doctrine. Evangelicals involved in renewal *are* concerned about doctrine. But they place priority on love, seeing Jesus' own priority stressed in the New Commandment. They believe firmly that growth is often a matter of time. That is, as a person is loved and accepted, the Holy Spirit will minister to him and bring his understanding in harmony with Truth. Thus, resistance to making an issue of doctrine is not rooted in heterodoxy, but in the firm conviction that within the body an atmosphere of love and valuing of persons creates the context in which growth in Truth, and toward maturity, can take place.

Certainly in those churches where marked renewal is present, a firm and practical commitment to the Word of God is clearly in evidence.

Challenged

The views just sketched have been presented often in recent years. And the challenge to prove whether a local church built on these principles will be effective has been raised.

In one sense, the challenge is tragically out of place. As conservatives, we have laid claim to being a people of the Book. God's Word has been affirmed as our rule and guide of life. It follows, then, that the *right* challenge is indeed "show me." But it is "show me *in the Word!*" Certainly the final standard we must apply to the approaches of both the Big Churches and renewal is the test of Scripture. And this is a test which renewal writers in particular have been careful to apply.

In another sense, the challenge is also deceptive. Too often the cry to "show me" means "show me that the principles you propose can build as big a church as we can following our principles!" This is deceptive because renewal does not view size or numbers as "the" criterion of success. What we need to do is to define the criteria by which church health is measured. When we have done this, *then* we can evaluate the effectiveness of both the Big Church and the renewal church using a variety of parameters including, but in addition to, size.

Finally, there is a sense in which the request to "show me" is an eminently fair one. The Word of God claims to describe reality. What Scripture presents is not idealistic, unrealistic, and "ivory tower." What Scripture presents must be seen by

God's people as practical and realistic. *We can expect, and have a right to demand, measurable results when principles of the Word of God are followed.* Thus, if renewal does reflect the teaching of Scripture about the church more accurately than the Big Church movement, then evidence should exist of both the practicality and effectiveness of these principles in operation in the ongoing life of many local churches.

I think this kind of evidence has been, and is being, presented. To the growing mass of this evidence I would like to add the story of three churches. Three churches, each distinctively different from the others. And each yet the same: the same in that the life of each is rooted deeply in the renewal principles revealed in the Word of God. Three churches, which demonstrate in their uniqueness the potential of every local church . . . of your local church . . . to become.

Part I « THE CHURCHES

In which we look at the differences
which exist, and the parallel principles
on which the life of each is built.

2 « Our Heritage: the revolutionary church

Paul, one of the "ministry team" (elders) at Our Heritage Church in Scottsdale, Arizona, sums up five years of renewal focus this way: "Coming to Our Heritage and going through the revolutionary process the church has gone through, it hasn't been a bed of roses. We've had our problems too. But I think the last couple of years especially have really opened up my life spiritually, and I don't know exactly how to describe it."

Our Heritage began full grown. A mission church of the Wesleyan Methodists, its buildings were ready before the first service began. That first Sunday, some two hundred people attended, and from that launching the church continued to maintain itself and grow. The pastor, Bob Girard, is a strong and gifted man: an exciting preacher and evangelist.

During the first two years of the church's life, some two hundred people came to know Christ through his pulpit and personal ministries. Looking back on those days, one of the elders recalls, "When the whole thing started off, Pastor Bob came on like a ball of fire. He would work his twenty hours a day from five in the morning to one in the morning, and he knew that if he worked hard enough, it would be successful. And he was dynamic. He has a strong personality, and he knew what he wanted. He knew what he was doing, and at first when we started off, we got into some real hassles. Bob knew exactly how things should be done, and all these other people knew exactly how things should be done."

Even with friction, the church grew. Soon there were graded choirs, boys and girls club activities, youth programs and activities — all the things we traditionally associate with a growing church.

Yet during those years Pastor Bob knew increasing personal dissatisfaction and unease. He saw people becoming Christians — but remaining babes! Bob Girard had asked for the new work, so that he might build a New Testament church. What he discovered he had was a twentieth-century American church just like the ones he had tried to run from. He shares one incident from those days:

"I came home one Sunday, back when we were still concerned about numbers, and was quite frustrated. I guess this was six or seven years ago. I was frustrated because it was a bad Sunday, so to speak, because there weren't as many people there as usual. I came home and I picked up the Bible, and I sat down, and you know, I was just thoroughly frustrated. I opened the Bible — and I don't very often just open and read — and looked down and right before me it said, 'And David counted the men and sinned against God.' And I said, 'Oh, Lord, I'm sorry.' I was worried about those empty pews, but what about the people in the pews? That's where we need to be concerned."

The people in the pews

The revolution brought about at Our Heritage since that time has focused on ministry to the people *in* the pews. Audrey Girard, Bob's wife, talks about the church today:

"I feel it's a church built around caring for the individual person. It's not built around programs, though they come into it as you share and work together. But the basic caring is for what goes on inside other people, and how you can help them find their way to the Lord and their life in the Lord. To find their way to the Lord is only beginning. Teaching them how to grow together and to share together the life that there is in Christ — that's what the church is all about."

Today the pattern of life and program at Our Heritage differ greatly from those early days. It reflects the shift to focus on building believers. The early thrust on programs has been replaced, and the old programs have largely disappeared.

The church meets together as a congregation on Sunday morning for an extended, informal service. Following a 9:30

Sunday school that offers special study topics for adults and instruction for youth and children, adults and teens gather in the sanctuary. The worship service grows spontaneously out of the experiences of the week, with music and sharing initiated by the congregation. Pastor Bob preaches — normally it's no sermonette! — and the congregation has opportunity to respond with questions, comments, or exhortations based on his ministry of the Word. Then the family, still together, shares joys and sorrows and needs, reporting answers to prayer and giving requests. The service usually lasts about two hours, with younger children cared for during this time in the small educational wing of the property.

This morning service, in which the whole body gathers, is significant to the life of the church. Just as significant are the "little churches" that meet in homes during the week. At present, approximately 70 percent of the Our Heritage people meet weekly in these small house-churches for Bible study, prayer, and sharing. These groups are open to members of other churches as well and have been vital in discipling new believers won to Christ through the witness of Our Heritage people. Joan, Paul's wife, sees them this way:

"Through the small group the body reaches out and brings in other people who would not otherwise be involved in Christian fellowship. I'm thinking particularly of my women's Bible study on Wednesday mornings. Many of the women are married to nonbelievers, and it's the only place they can come and discuss the Word. It's the only place where they can share problems in love and know that everyone there is concerned about them and their relationship to Christ. I believe too that the strength of the small groups lies in the prayers that go up.

"Our Wednesday group draws from I don't know how many congregations. I can think of at least six denominations. But I think every one of us involved goes back to our churches and spreads the Word there to other people."

The building ministry of the "little churches" is one of the factors that makes the Sunday service so rich and meaningful, as the spiritual growth stimulated there is reflected in the sharing of the brothers and sisters while the congregation gathers for worship.

These two settings — the congregation gathered together, and the congregation gathered in "little churches" during the week — are the only regular meetings now held for the people of Our Heritage. Beyond these two meeting settings, which focus on growth through mutual love and encouragement in the Word, believers at Our Heritage are encouraged to be involved with their neighbors, with their families, and in living "in the world," to share Christ with those around them.

Youth ministry

As soon as the emaciated "program" of Our Heritage is described, people ask about youth. "Don't you have programs for your teens? What about them?"

Ron Rogers, the youthful, long-haired associate of Bob Girard's at Our Heritage, concentrates on ministry with young people. Converted while in college in 1965, Ron has "grown up" as a Christian in the church and as a part of its ministry. His approach to youth ministry, while initially in the traditional "activity" pattern, has changed as the church's emphasis has changed. He describes the present emphasis as "just pouring your life into a couple of guys."

Ron does plan infrequent Sunday evening "youth thing" activities for teens, who need to meet each other in informal social settings. But the heart of the ministry is found in the several "little churches" of teens and young teens that meet during the week, in the daily meetings Ron has with individuals to build them, in simple witnessing on the high-school campuses, and in the full participation of teens in the body-life meeting of the congregation.

Of the teens presently involved, Ron says, "They really love one another, and I think we're beginning to see in the fellowship of the small group that we have a commitment to one another, to the point where I think they would be willing to die for one another. I really do."

Asked to describe their commitment, Ron responds: "You can go to any evangelical church in Phoenix and Scottsdale, and you can find kids in whom Christ is really alive. But I would say, the thing I see with our kids is that with the majority of them, Christ is a living part of their daily lives. They can relate Him to their problems. He is really an integral, vital part of their lives, and it's not at all equated with do's and don'ts.

"I want to take that one step further. Christ is not only a very vital part of their lives, He *is* their lives. At school it's a relationship with Jesus, at home it's a relationship with Jesus, and it's a constant dependence on Him as a person that makes them different."

Right now at Our Heritage the number of youth involved is down. Part of the reason is that a large number of seniors went off to college at the same time, and a very high percentage — about fifty or sixty — are planning for full-time ministry.

The slow "build people" rather than "reach masses" approach at first led to misunderstandings with some parents of teens. But the quality of the ministry has largely overcome these today. Youth are a vital and exciting part of the church as a whole, full and fellow members with the adults in the adventure of growing together in this revolutionary church.

Hang it up

Ron Rogers is speaking. "I was talking with a brother yesterday for about seven hours, and he said the one thing he admires more than anything else about Bob is the courage he has to put into practice the things he sees in Jesus' theory. There are probably thousands of ministers around who believe and feel exactly the same way Bob does, but they're not willing to hang it up and get cut off."

The willingness of the pastor and church to *risk* is one of the things that marks off Our Heritage in its revolutionary course. One example of this willingness is in finances; the pastors led the people into striking changes based on a determination to let the Holy Spirit direct and guide the life of this portion of Christ's church. The present situation, according to Bob Girard, just "evolved."

"At each point I can go only so far as I can see something in the Word. Once I saw it, or Ron saw, or somebody else saw it, we began teaching on it," Girard says.

"Well, in the area of finances, we began teaching that the New Testament didn't necessarily teach tithing. Rather, there was something higher and better. We began then on the same basis to remove all pressure on people to give a certain amount or to pledge. This was something to let God lead them in, and motives are as important as what is done — this is where it started.

The next year — well, every spring we always presented our budget. I then preached a message in contradiction to the whole thing. I talked about some of the principles of support of Christian workers and so forth, and I began teaching without saying how it ought to be done. It was teaching that probably in passing the offering plate just put people under pressure, and it was a fleshly thing, because every time we talked about it with the board, it was always, 'If you don't, people are not going to remember.'

"One of our laymen suggested that if we were just going to let the Holy Spirit do it and not set up a budget to aim for, then maybe we ought to take steps of faith as a church. The first step of faith was to take 10 percent off the top to give away to other ministries. Another step came when we elected a committee to pray about our financial needs instead of talk about how far behind we were at every board meeting.

"About two years ago," Pastor Bob continued, "Ron and I and our families talked about it. I had been preaching some sermons again about the Christian worker being dependent on the Father instead of on the church treasury, so he was responsible to the Father instead of the board. We decided that we had had enough hassle about back finances and that the Lord was talking to us about trusting Him. We came to the board with the proposal that they pay everything else first and us last, if there were anything left. And if there were, they would divide it proportionately, depending on the need of our family. We would trust God to supply all our needs, as He promised to do in Philippians 4:19.

"The board members didn't like the idea at all. It took us two months to convince them, and finally they said, 'Okay, if these guys are convinced that this is what they ought to do, it's ridiculous, but we'll try it.' Immediately all the church bills were paid. And immediately our salary wasn't. For the first eighteen months we got full salary only about three times.

"At the end of that eighteen-month period, all our family bills were paid. Never before in twenty-four years of marriage had all our bills been paid. The Lord had supplied our needs, sometimes in fantastic ways.

"For the last eight months we've received full salary. An offering is never taken during the worship service, but rather at the door, and finances have come up. The whole experience has made a difference in the life of our family — we now know what trust is. And in the church board too."

After this interview, giving suddenly fell at Our Heritage. Today the board is studying together what God is seeking to communicate. The possibility is being explored that the Lord may be indicating His desire that the buildings be sold (building costs take up more than 50 percent of the church's budget) and the money invested in freeing other men to minister, and in meeting the needs of brothers and sisters as the New Testament definitely encourages.

One thing seems certain. The church, following the example of its spiritual leaders, has through the years come to the place where the majority are willing to risk and to follow the wise advice of Mary: "Whatsoever *he* saith unto you, do it!" (John 2:5 KJV).

3 « Mariners: the church with freedom to be

It's fun to hear Mariners' people talking about their church. "The Thanksgiving Morning service really typifies this church," Lawana is saying. "I was in tears at the end of it. Bill led it. It was at eight o'clock. The church was almost filled, and Bill got up and sat on a stool in front. Bill said, 'I am not prepared for this service, purposely. This is your service.'

"Everything there was spontaneous, everything was sharing, there was never a minute's hesitation, there was never a time when there weren't at least two people standing. It was new to me, and it's the most impressive thing I've ever been in.

"People would say, 'Okay, let's sing such and such.' Or, 'I'd like to ask Fay to sing a solo.' One man had a whole bunch of notes and he said, 'I took a poll last night in the household to see what we were thankful for,' and read them off. Another fellow got up crying and said, 'I want you to know that my father called me two times today, inviting me to Thanksgiving dinner,' and added, 'I've been having so much trouble communicating with my father.' This sort of thing. We were all just absolutely dissolved into tears at the end of it, and a couple of the board members came and hugged me and told me how glad they were that I was here and it was the neatest experience ever. I think it typifies this church."

A new Christian says, "When we used to run on the cocktail circuit, we would make phony conversations and get next to people who you think will do you some good. But people accept you here at our church. Accept you the way you are. They're really friendly, and they care about your spiritual growth, and they make sure you are growing. If you have a problem, well, they just come right out and we share problems here. If someone is hurting, there is always someone to call or someone calls you. And if you have marital problems or children problems, you can share them with other people. We come together all the time, to share our lives and where we have needs. I've never experienced anything like it.

"You know, you attend churches where you go Sunday morning and Sunday night — and if you're spiritual, Wednesday — and if you're really great you get to teach Sunday school. But you don't really talk to many other people. Here we have people over to dinner. Or I go to a prayer meeting, and it's really a prayer meeting where people have needs and share them. We meet in homes for Bible studies where we pray for one another and try to apply the Word to our lives. This is an entirely different life from any church I've been in."

Bob picks up the now-familiar theme. "I have more freedom with people than I did previously. It came about with a greater understanding through the Word of who I am and the ability to accept myself. And it came about when people accepted me as I am. I think acceptance in this fellowship is so great that you don't have to come in with any masks. You just come in as you are."

Traditional?

In some ways, Mariners looks like a bustling traditional church. There are three Sunday morning services, made necessary by the explosive growth of the fellowship from about 250 to 750 in the past two and a half or three years. There is a (small) Sunday evening service. There is a three-man pastoral staff, with duties focusing on preaching, counseling, and youth. There is a well-organized Sunday school. And there are plans for building — a building to seat two thousand with many multipurpose facilities for the expanded ministries the church board foresees for the congregation in the community. These plans range from a community resource and counseling center, on through dormitory space for Christian students at the nearby branch of the University of California, on to the welcome to be given to various community organizations for use of the facilities.

Throughout the planning of this half-million-dollar expansion there is the conviction that to continue with its unique ministry, Mariners must remain a church where people are accepted, welcomed into each other's lives, and enabled to grow. The personal dimension and the warmth that makes Mariners a place where people sense freedom to be, and to become, is something board and pastor are convinced must never be lost.

Mariners Church was begun with no thought of becoming what it is today: a congregation with an increasingly great impact on the wealthy Newport Beach, California, community in which it's located, and increasingly great size. Bob and Nayda tell about its early beginnings:

"During the first eight or ten years of my Christian life," says Bob, "I grew under some great Bible teaching, with a healthy emphasis on doctrinal teaching. But there was not much expression of love in the body and not much expression of the work of Christ in the world. So in 1958 when Lloyd and Jackie moved into our area and joined our fellowship, they brought a freshness into the church. They had been involved in home Bible classes, which was really new at the time, and some of us got involved. I was among four other men and our wives who simultaneously thought we should get something going in an interdenominational church to be free to gather and study God's Word and share with each other."

Nayda picks up the story: "We were really concerned that we were being led away from our old fellowship involvement that we were very active in and not even feeling that dissatisfied with. We went one Saturday morning to Lloyd and Jackie's and said, 'We need you guys to pray for us about something, because we're concerned about our attitudes, and what we feel is a sense of being divorced from the church without knowing why.' So we prayed about it, because they were experiencing the same kind of thing.

"We realized within a few days that it also was happening to the Kings and the Saffells and the Weamers, and we got together within a week and were just overwhelmed at the possibility that God had separated us and begun to reveal Himself to us like this. It was overwhelming, because we weren't clear as to what it was going to be, but we knew He was doing it. It's been that way ever since.

"That's why it was so great that the guys met to think and pray. They weren't meeting as a committee. They were just waiting on the Lord. He would give them an insight, and they would move on it.

"We tried to go back to our church and share this. It didn't make sense to them, and a lot of people didn't understand us, and tried to think why we were splitting up, and, you know, how many families were going with us. We said, 'No, it's not that. There's no dissatisfaction in that sense. It's just that God has led us, and you can think of us as a mission church.' It was something we couldn't describe, yet we knew it was what God wanted, and we simply acted in obedience to it."

Today the men of those original families, with a few added, constitute the governing board of the church, which is a permanent board and has authority to make all decisions involving the congregation. In the ten years since Mariners Church became a reality, many changes have taken place with growth. But the basic principle on which the leadership operates is still the same: The Lord will give an insight, and they will move on it.

The pastor

In most ways, the role that Bob Girard played in shaping the early life of Our Heritage Church has been played by the entire board at Mariners. Still, much of the impact of the church today can be traced to Mariners' youthful pastor, Joe Aldrich, who came to Newport Beach in 1971 after completing his doctoral studies at Dallas Theological Seminary. Joe's preaching ministry reinforces the atmosphere of acceptance and welcome, and his personality blends with those of the church's leaders.

Coming to Mariners, Joe found "a group of men who had a vision of ministering and of commitment to each other. That," he says, "is probably the strangest single concept of the ministry that we had: That we existed to meet each other's needs, and that we encourage, uplift, and build each other."

What does Joe see as his pastoral function in a church that

is essentially run by its elders? "Primarily as pastor-teacher. I see myself primarily as teaching at the church gathering. I spend a lot of time with the men during the week. I try to have three or four luncheon appointments a week with the men, trying to encourage and find out where they're at. This hasn't been easy, or something I did naturally. After I had been here eight months or so they asked me, Why haven't you established more significant relationships with the board members? Now it's more of a disciplining ministry, and in my own estimation my Sunday morning ministry is taking on less significance."

Joe tells of growth through the ministry of the church to him — growth in ability to communicate, ability to minister and accept ministry. From conversation with the people of the church, it's clear that Joe's ministry is a vitally important factor in the life of the body. Individuals speak of his counseling and personal impact. Nearly all speak of his preaching.

But again and again people return to the theme of the accepting, open climate of the fellowship, and of the care they sense for each other. "Never, in the two years I've been intimately involved here, have I seen or heard of anyone who has been turned off to any significant degree," Dave says. "I mean, just knowing people the way I know them, there's a spirit here that makes people stop and think. I see one man here every Sunday, a very successful attorney. I know his wife persuades him to come, and he's strong enough that if it weren't for the spirit of this church and that attitude, he'd say 'No way.' But there's a spirit here."

Another person says, "I really think the fellowship we have with the Christians is probably the most exciting part of the church. The exciting part of our Christian growth is the changes we've seen in our own lives."

This personal dimension reflects the original and continuing commitment of the board. "I think the board feels that we cannot expect anything deeper to happen in the lives of our church body than is happening in our own board members," says Joe Aldrich. "So if we want to develop quality relationships in our family, we have to do it ourselves. They really take that seriously."

The board members are also exposed as men to the members of the body, for each one teaches in the church. In particular, they take turns assisting in a class required of all prospective members. Board families are involved in small groups — not just with each other, but with other families. Sunday morning services are led by the board members rather than the pastor. The board also takes seriously the responsibility of governing and disciplining in the fellowship and is often involved in the lives of individuals needing support or correction.

The personal dimension is also reflected in Joe Aldrich's preaching. To the church board members, "the proclamation of Christ and His Word is the single most important strength the church has." Joe's preaching ministry focuses on helping people develop inner qualities of maturity that mark them off as Jesus' own.

"In the three years here, I've learned to be more simple," Joe explains. "And more explicit, coming up with behavioral objectives. I think of what I want them to feel and what I want them to do and what I want them to know. I key off with a phrase they've heard probably one thousand times: if we commit ourselves to truth, the product is always beauty. It may take a while, but it will always be beauty in human relationships. Relationships within the body, the mutuality of ministry, and so on. I probably preach little to church needs, but am more personal. The messages are particularly directed toward the concept that the Spirit's purpose is to glorify Christ, and every provision has been made for life and godliness in the Spirit. So I've been thinking in messages more in terms of family, relational needs rather than teachings about the church as a body."

This emphasis is something the people seem to appreciate. "Joe's major role?" one responded, "To really pastor the flock, teach us, and if we get hung up, he can pop open the Scripture and give us the Word and pray with us about it."

In this church — where pastors and board members are deeply committed to love, acceptance, and care for people — it seems only natural that the life of fellowship, accepting one another, and extending real freedom to be oneself and grow as God gives the increase, should be the distinguishing marks of a dynamic, growing body.

4 « Trinity: church of the believer-priests

The formula is on the Trinity Church letterhead: **PW**$_2$. Praise, Worship, and Work. This provides the pattern for the life of this ten-year-old church in Seattle, Washington.

Talking to the pastor of those ten years, Gib Martin, you quickly get the impression that this church isn't like the other two. Rather, God has taken the same principles of life and shaped this body uniquely.

We hear some of the differences that make Trinity unique in statements like these by Gib:

"I think we have presumed that people would be discipled by the morning message, by structuring a few classes. But disciples do not happen. Jesus said, 'Make disciples.' . . .

"We're not building our church around small groups or Bible studies, and we don't even want that kind of language spread around here. We are building our whole concept around a discipleship principle that says if you are a disciple, you are reaching maturity and you do serve, so ours is built on service, and not groups or studies or things like that. . . .

"To me, even in the clutter of the church today, I find it to be a beautiful thing. I find beauty in the church of Jesus Christ, and to me it's terribly exciting to find Christ shining through the eyes of my brother and my sister. . . .

"Pastors are leaders when they identify with the people, mingle with the flock, are a part of the flock. We see ourselves as sheep under the great high Shepherd. So if I ever lose my 'sheephood,' I hope I will be escorted quickly to the gate. It's despicable to develop another clerical system, and it's easy, be-

30

cause people want to make you a pope. But I'm only one living stone, and I have to keep reminding myself of that."

Ten years

Like Mariners Church, Trinity began ten years ago, when five families came together. Today Virginia, who was among those first couples, laughs as she looks back on the beginnings: "I am amused, because the first concept of our church was that we were going to be a cultural church to the up-and-outers — and the Lord has taken it in exactly opposite directions."

The Grapevine. Begun as a coffee shop in the late sixties, the Grapevine has become a living and learning center that puts into practice the Matthew 25 grace of reaching out with the cup of cold water and visiting those in prison. Today a staff of five handles the more then nine hundred calls for help that come to the Grapevine each month. The widows of the church have formed a group called the Grapevine Auxiliary. They not only have taken over meeting basic physical needs, such as planning balanced meals for the residents at the Grapevine, but also "have a positive influence on the kids and the behavior of the people who live there."

Today the five-point program of the Grapevine meets medical and psychological needs, caring for the person "as a body before you deal with him as a spirit — and get rid of his toothache and his eye problems, venereal disease, and whatever else is hanging him up so that he can't think about anything else. Get rid of the pain that he's suffering, and from the foolishness that he's involved in."

Ivan, Pat, and Susan, whom you will meet in Chapter Twelve, give you some insight into the impact of the Grapevine ministry.

Sky Club. Gary, an airline pilot, was jolted one day coming back from a softball game when Gib asked him, "Gary, if you could do anything you wanted with your life, what would you do?" Gary shared a dream: a dream of reaching boys through flight — building model aircraft and electronics.

Gib and Gary began to pray, money was raised, and today, after a three-year pilot program, more than two thousand persons are involved in several states and even in Indonesia. Focusing on the personal relationship developed between the men who are "big brothers" to the boys involved, the ministry draws to Christ and moves on to first steps in discipleship.

Study center. The evangelistic ministry of the Grapevine, along with other ministries that began to draw young, new Christians to the body at Trinity, pointed up a new need. A need for a place of discipline and training in discipleship.

Gib explains: "First we started a coed house, and we gave assignments. The people who lived there had to be through high school, and they had to be willing to submit to the church and the board of elders. They had to pay their own way to be there. We made it difficult: the people who came were people who really wanted to stay.

"If people do not need to work to support themselves, they have to work for somebody in the church or community. Take care of somebody. Paint a widow's house for her. They study three or four hours a day and write weekly papers. Then the board of elders and their wives come to the study center itself, and the papers are read and reviewed. The young people are examined for the content of their theology, and for how practical it was in terms of their own person.

"You can just see the kids grow. Two of the boys are entering seminary next year who were in our first study group. One girl had come off the drug scene, and it opened up a whole new dimension of life. She is now a secretary to a doctor, doing an unbelievably good job, and her life is stabilized. Each person who has been through the study center approach has come out a strong and growing disciple."

Today the church is planning for two study centers — one for guys and one for gals — and something new: an art center, to encompass all the graphic arts, to help Christian artists develop. Gib says, "That's part of discipling the gifts for the glory of the body. Artists have never really had a significant place in the body of Christ. They've drawn Sunday school papers and things like that. But we want to move into the fine arts and give them a universal ministry."

Survival Bible training. Ken, who heads up the development of Survival Bible training, has been in the church for several years. Today many members work with him in production of this in-depth, discipling Bible study approach for use with older teens, training them in how to study and use Scripture in daily living. The program has been tested and revised several times and is now being used in the Seattle area; it is available for wider use.

Ken says of the church, "It has been the central influence in my life, and the materials being developed under the authority of the Trinity Church board of elders are an expression of the Trinity family. There are about fifty people actively involved in the production of the materials and in the operation of the courses. Without Trinity Church there would be no Survival Bible training."

Missions. This is another emphasis of Trinity the Body. A dozen missionaries represent the church, as it has taken on an average of a little better than one for each year of its existence. In all, the budget for the church, missions, the Grapevine, Sky Club, the study center, and Survival Bible training runs to more then $100,000 — for 141 heads of families!

Priests. The real distinctiveness of the ministry, however, is not seen even in its structured ministries. It lies in the development of each member as a priest, serving others and the community.

Mila heads a women's Bible study that involves teaching four hundred women weekly, with forty leaders. She says, "I never intended to be in a position like this, but the Lord does those kinds of things. I think that going to Trinity prepared me for it in the freedom I find there. We have to allow for certain different thoughts in the Bible Study Fellowship and give people freedom in that situation. That's what I learned at Trinity — that we're not just one church that's right and all the others are wrong."

Of the motivation to serve, Don, another believer-priest in the community, says, "People here really believe. As Gib says, 'We don't just believe *in* God, we believe *God!*'" A wholehearted trust in God, an awareness that Christ is coming, a love for people — these have moved all the men and women of Trinity to minister.

A slow process

Trinity has grown into what it is through ten years of struggling to sense and respond to God's leading. Gib came out of

Catholicism and points out that originally he had no vision of being a pastor, and no polity. While this has been a disadvantage in some ways, today Gib says, "I believe the advantage is that I have been willing to risk what others always seem to want to protect."

What happened during the ten years, and how has Trinity grown? "The ministry went very slowly during the first years because of the healing that had to take place," Gib responds. "We went through three phases of growth. We began as a spirit. There was a desire, and that was all; that spirit was all we were for three years. We were so fragmented — people were not really capable of handling anything emotional. The aim of my first three years here was just to be a friend and pastor and teacher, to nurture so as to help the people get rid of feelings of antagonism, frustration, and so on.

"In the next three or four years we became a soul. We actually took shape. But we were not yet a body. There were a lot of individuals who knew Jesus Christ, because we were beginning to grow and to multiply. But it was not yet a very beautiful thing.

"Then in the last three years we have become a body. We're a body, and there's great affection and trust, and an animation of truth."

This has not been Gib's work alone. Though in many ways his teaching of the Word and his vision have been used to shape the life of the church, Gib recalls, "I took seriously the statement in Joel and Acts 2. God will pour out His Spirit on all flesh, young and old. I say God put together an older generation, in terms of our board, and a younger generation, in terms of myself and our staff. I saw them dreaming together, and blending. They helped shape me, because my enthusiasm sometimes ran ahead. I helped to inspire them and encourage them. It was a beautiful combination of actors."

Earlier I spoke of Trinity as the "church of the believer-priest." This thrust in the ministry there has helped to shape the body. "When I opened up the concept that every believer is a priest, that every believer is to minister, and that I am an under-servant to the servants — it brought about a strange reaction for a year. There was no concept of that at all. I began almost to harp on it, to the point where people would laugh at this word *priest*. I would call them priests — 'How's my fellow priest today?' and all that sort of thing. Little ways to lift the word out of the context of Scripture.

"Something began to happen. The Holy Spirit of God caused the people to believe this. You see, it was no gimmick. In my heart I did not believe it was a gimmick, and the Lord honored my faith to resurrect this truth. I spent time in Hebrews and 1 Peter 2 and other passages to get this in perspective. After this completely saturated the minds of the believers, the Lord began to speak to my heart and the hearts of several others about gifts. And so the vision grew. I launched into two years of immersing the minds of the body in the gift concept and exploring it together.

"Out of this, and while this was happening, God was giving visions to men and women in the church, so I took on a heavy discipling ministry." Today most of the men and women you meet at Trinity speak of the discipling emphasis stressed by Gib and the other leaders.

The point, of course, is clear. Trinity and other renewal churches do not spring full-blown from a weekend retreat. Nor are they produced by some new formula for instant "success." Renewal is the shaping of the body of Christ by the Spirit of God. And this shaping — touching attitudes and concepts and perspectives, reworking feelings and emotions and relationships, blending and welding individuals into a body — takes time and takes openness to the leading of God. Perhaps above all for pastor and board, renewal takes the willingness to risk.

Together

Even looked at externally, Trinity isn't a "normal" church. It meets now, as it has for a number of years, in a mortuary. Morning services are constructed to be both love and teaching services, with love experienced and expressed. On Sunday evenings two-hour Schools of Christian Living provide unique training and experience of biblical concepts critical to growth and ministry. Midweek EPIC (Everyone Praying in Concert) features a meal together and then prayer time.

Parents are urged to make the evening meal a family love feast. Love is shown in the intensive counseling ministry carried on through the church. Besides time with the church family, Gib himself meets with twenty-five couples a week for family and marriage counseling, and he has a long waiting list. The two secretaries who give their time and Mark, the director of the Grapevine, serve as comforters. Jean, the young woman who serves as church administrator, is another person with love's "tender touch."

Although not encouraging the kind of small groups characteristic of the other two churches, the same relationships of love are built in the task and ministry groups of Trinity. Describing a typical planning meeting, Mila says, "There are about seven of us. We usually meet at my house and have coffee. We visit a bit, actually, about things happening in our lives and families and church. And we have quite a good time of prayer for one another and for people in the church having trouble. Then we go through the practical details of planning meetings."

Gib sees this gathering in ministry groups as a strength: people are driven to the Word and to prayer as they plan for their ministries. Each of the ministry groups at Trinity has developed a deep, close, and loving relationship.

Of Sky Club, Bob, a new believer, says, "I actually feel a love relationship between Gary and me, because I know that he loves me in spite of myself because the Lord loves me. I look at board meetings as more than just discussing business. It's a time when we can fellowship together and learn a little bit about each other, and what God is doing in our lives, and any problems. It's as much a time of fellowship as business."

This, plus the intimate one-on-one relationships that seem so common at Trinity, mark its fellowship with the same distinctive family feeling that is perhaps the most quickly distinguished mark of churches which are deep into evangelical renewal.

Arrived

One of the concerns of the board at Trinity as I spoke with them about this book was that some readers might see them as, in some ways, having "arrived." The men are deeply aware of what God has been doing — and all are deeply aware that their body has only begun to scratch the surface of His possibilities.

This is a healthy attitude. It's one we all need to take, whatever the place we find ourselves in. God is a Person who opens up all of life to us and invites us to expect Him to do great things in our lives and fellowship. Wherever we may be, there is yet much more for us to possess — and to possess us.

Keeping an attitude of expectancy, opening ourselves up to God and to His direction, can help us to experience in our future the fullest meaning of renewal.

5 « Spiritual leadership

One of the threads that draws together the experience of the three churches and gives them a commonness and unity, is their understanding of leadership. Each draws on a uniquely biblical concept — servant leadership — and each expresses this in practical ways.

The servant-leader

The demand for a unique kind of leadership in the body of Christ is expressed clearly by the Lord in Matthew 20. There, speaking of the rulers of the heathen who lord it over their subjects and have absolute power, Jesus insisted, "It must not be so among you. No, whoever among you wants to be great must become your servant, and if he wants to be first among you he must be your slave — just as the Son of Man has not come to be served but to serve, and to give his life to set many others free" (vv. 26-28).

The two contrasting models of leadership — the one which the church must embrace and the other which it must reject — contain many significant comparisons and contrasts. In both cases, *leadership* is exercised. The secular ruler is not "strong" while the servant-leader is "weak." Both are strong: both involve men with authority who provide leadership and give focus to the lives and experiences of others around them.

Yet the contrasts are many. First, there is the contrast of relationship. The pagan ruler "lords it *over*" others. The servant-leader is "among" them. Second, there is the contrast of attitude. Secular authority has brought others into conformity, as it imposes its will. But the servant-leader seeks to free others and to give himself for others' benefit. The secular ruler has absolute power and uses the sanctions of power to impose his will and bring about conformity. The servant-leader has no such external power; sanctions, such as punishment or reduction in wages, are not available to him. Instead, his power is a dynamic, internal thing, which touches the wellsprings of motive and leads the follower to a self-chosen commitment. Last, there is a difference in method. The secular ruler *tells* others what to do. The servant, unable to command, *does* — and in the doing demonstrates.

It is in this, the power of example, that the servant's ability to motivate others is exercised. Peter speaks to his fellow elders and points out, "You should aim not at being dictators but examples of Christian living in the eyes of the flock committed to your charge (1 Peter 5:3). Paul encourages the Philippians, "That which you have heard and seen in me do, and the God of peace will be with you" (Phil. 4:9). Spiritual leadership serves others, seeking to free them to reveal the beauty of Jesus; in conjunction with the Word, the secret of such leadership is summed up in the power of example. In the incarnating of Truth taught, so that its reality can be seen in a human life, the call to commitment is communicated from heart to heart.

Visiting the three churches, you notice differences in organization. Differences in the way the boards function; differences of gift in the pastors. But in each, the dynamic of spiritual leadership and its underlying principles remain the same!

Our Heritage

From its inception Our Heritage has been an expression of the vision and the personality of Bob Girard. For years, Pastor Bob has been "the leader," and the body has expressed both his strengths — and his weaknesses. Recently a change has begun. Today the concept of multiple, local lay leadership is being implemented with a "Ministry Team" (which corresponds to the elders of most churches) and an "Associates in Ministry" board. The goal is to develop within the fellowship a team of leaders who can together experience what God desires for the body, and then increasingly model this for the church.

In the process, the lay leaders are taking increasingly significant roles in church services and planning. On Saturday mornings the ministry team meets for three hours to study together
Scripture that relates to the life and direction of the body. Each
member is also involved in small groups. The need of leaders to
be committed to each other, to grow in their capacity to mirror
the truths which God wants to build into the experience of the
body, is just being recognized — and the experience of building
together begun.

Yet, in many ways lay leadership has been continually demonstrated in this distinctive church. If we understand spiritual
leadership as providing an example, as revealing in human
personality the meaning of the freedom God calls us to, this
church has been rich in leadership. Each Sunday's sharing by
members of God's work in their lives has set a spiritual pace
and has motivated all to a deeper trust in God and to a greater
expectancy.

Mariners

This church teaches us many lessons about leadership. One
lesson is in the way that the church board — a permanent board
of men selected for life — rules the body.

A secretary there comments, "One thing that excites me about
the church is that Joe Aldrich isn't running it. There are eight
men I talk with several times a week. When I first started working here, I called a board member and felt really guilty about
disturbing him about church business. Then I realized that the
board members feel it *is* their business. Knowing the inside
workings of this church is exciting, knowing that these men
pray for this church and give abundantly of their time."

When I learned how absolute is the control of the board over
the church, I probed to see how other members felt about the
"benevolent oligarchy," as I initially characterized it. Does
this kind of leadership rule out meaningful participation by
others in the church? The answer that emerges is complex.
*People are not cut off from the significant life of the church,
for significance is not found in board and committees and program, but in reaching out to love and care for people.* When believers sense God's touch in their own lives, and through them

in the lives of others, the *mechanics* of church become unimportant! In this, by the way, the board actually takes the servant role. They do the necessary work organizationally to make sure that the body is free to respond to the needs of people! In caring for the church, they serve the servants and enable them to minister to real needs.

Another dimension of the answer comes in communication. The board at Mariners is not isolated from the people, but is *among* them. The board members listen. As the conviction of need for a building program grew, the board communicated its concern and concepts. The church members were given questionnaires and asked to express opinions and feelings. All this information became part of the prayer concern of the leaders, who were and are committed to serving the people of the body. The success of the men in listening both to God and to His people is seen in the fact that the 750 members (98 percent) of the body have expressed full agreement with the plan for building shared with them by the board.

A third insight came when I asked the board members how they keep from becoming despots. Their answer? "We discipline each other." The men of the board take responsibility not only for the body, but also for the relationship of each other with God and the body. This in-depth commitment helps keep them individually and as a whole in sensitive touch with the Spirit of God, who as agent for the Head of the Body communicates Christ's will.

I asked numerous members of the congregation about the church leaders. Typical response? "How do they give leadership? They know that God has called them, and that alone gives me an assurance, as a person who is being led. I trust their relationship with each other, and their being obedient to the Holy Spirit."

Joe Aldrich reflects what the members feel when he says, "They have a tremendous role as behavioral models for the congregation. The people of this church hold them in esteem as examples." This role looms so large that, Joe continues, "I see my role and the board's role, our key responsibility, as maintaining unity among ourselves. I think Satan's first major challenge is to crack that board and bring division and disunity, and I pray it never happens."

Still another ministry of the board among the people — besides their participation in services, teaching, and small groups — is disciplining. The board views anything that touches the life of the members of the body as their concern, in terms of both the love the body needs to show its members, and the encouragement it needs to give for individual growth toward maturity. Asked how they get involved in the lives of the members, the board gave example after example — from giving time to advise brothers in business situations, to disciplining a man who was using the church to make contacts for questionable property deals, to correcting individuals who had fallen into sin.

Through it all, Joe's summarizing words have been validated over and over again. Here are men who are servants and examples. And whose primary commitment is expressed in all their activities within the body; a primary commitment Joe summarizes this way: "I think the board has the feeling that we cannot expect anything deeper to happen in the lives of our church body than what is happening in our own board. So if we want to develop quality relationships in our Family, we have to do it ourselves. And they really take that seriously."

They should. The servant-leader is the leader who *does* — and who in doing both shows the way and calls out an eager desire to follow in the hearts of those the Spirit of God is touching.

Trinity

Trinity, like Mariners, has a permanent board. Asked a question about dictatorship, the people at Trinity look surprised. "We don't have that situation," Virginia reacts. "Even to the youngest child, if they don't agree with something they're very vocal, and the men care. They may not agree, but they will listen and discuss this. There just isn't any 'this is my way and we will go this way, period.' " At Trinity, too, the people know the board members intimately, submit willingly to the authority of the Word of God, and know the hearts of their board members so completely that they trust them fully.

"A dictatorship could happen," Virginia muses, "if we were not Spirit led. Gib is a very dominant personality, and he has strong opinions. If he believes in something, if you disagree . . .

well, we have had those times when he disagrees with me, because he sets his jaw a certain way. But we're not intimidated."

Mark adds something here, something Gib demonstrates as well as the other board members. "We discipline each other. My discipline doesn't just come from the other elders, but from individual members around me. I think this is our experience. It is the body's concern for each other as brothers that kind of supersedes our oversight. There has to be a submitting to each other as part of the brotherly ministry of each of us."

The whole-hearted willingness to submit to one another is balanced by another theme heard often at Trinity — *authority*. The young find it easy — though often after a time of struggle! — to submit to the authority of the board and the pastor.

Ken speaks about the need for authority and leadership. "A key element in making the people of God usable is to find somebody — preferably an elder in your local church — whom you look up to spiritually to help you pattern the direction of your life's ministry. Without the aid of some human expression of God's pattern for this age, I don't think it's possible for a person to grow and thrive." Ken found this person in Gib: "I would not be sitting here if it were not for the ministry of Gib Martin as a servant to me. He served me for a good time before I came to the point where I submitted to his authority and was voluntarily under his authority in the development of my life's ministry."

The authority of the board members is exercised individually and as a group — over the many works of the church while they encourage and support and guide — over individuals in the study center and Grapevine ministries. This board also disciplines — itself first, and then others in the congregation. In March 1974 the board members accepted a new risk in leadership, and now each member has "office hours" at the church, taking on many of the counseling and other responsibilities once held only by the pastor.

Looking at leadership, Gib says, "Ninety-eight percent of the leader's responsibility is to believe in people long enough, until they believe in the one who believes in them, and then finally, until they're able to believe in themselves again." When they do believe in themselves again, this short history of Trinity suggests, they are free to accept their roles as believer-priests and to move into the lives of others through praise, worship, and work, the **PW₂** formula for life at Trinity.

Thinking about the part of the body which represents leaders, the people at Trinity have come to understand it as the foot. "We are the servant, and we should be the feet, with the body carrying out the ministry, and the Head, Jesus Christ, should be exalted. We've taken Romans 15:1-3 as our staff exhortation: 'We who are strong ought to bear with the failings of the weak, and not to please ourselves; let each of us please his neighbor for his good, to edify him. For Christ did not please himself; but, as it is written, "The reproaches of those who reproached thee fell on me" ' (RSV). So that has been our exhortation — that we are servant to the servants."

Leadership

Seen in the life of these three congregations, leadership seems full of strange contradictions. The leadership is strong and holds unusual authority in the church, yet the people never perceive their leaders as authoritarian. The leaders commit themselves to serve, yet the people they serve enjoy submitting to them. The leaders concentrate on building their own life's commitment, unity, and mutual growth, yet the unity and commitment demonstrated by the board are increasingly reflected in the congregation. The board members in the fullest sense are "over" the congregation, yet they are seen by the member as "among" them . . . and to themselves, the board members seem "under" the flock which they serve. The leadership makes decisions, yet the needs of all are heard and considered, and the decisions made are sensed as an expression of the will of both the Head and the Body.

Perhaps these paradoxes, impossible in the secular-ruler concept of leadership, are an integral part of the life of a body that is ruled by servants. Certainly Jesus, in cutting us off from the model of the secular ruler in such a blunt and absolute way ("it must not be so among you"), and in inviting us to experience the leadership of servants, opened the way to a new thing. His church, a body — an organism rather than an organization — has a distinct life all its own.

As renewal takes root in congregations around the country

and the world, the rediscovery of the meaning of servant-leader seems one of the vital conditions for a full experience of what it means to be *His* church.

6 « Family feeling

Jesus' initial words to His disciples on the occasion of the Last Supper — that time when, many believe, He gave the Constitution of the Church and seedbed of the New Testament revelation — were on a theme that is repeated over and over in the later epistles. *Love.*

"Now I am giving you a new command," John records Jesus as saying. "Love one another. Just as I have loved you, so you must love one another. This is how all men will know that you are my disciples, because you have such love for one another" (John 13:34, 35).

The concept of love is hardly new to Scripture. What is new, however, is the "one another" relationship to which it is applied. In the body which is His church, Jesus has welded believers into one. In the "one new man," we are even more intimately related than brothers and sisters. What is also new is the standard: we are no longer to love others as we love ourselves. Now believers, united in Jesus to one another, are to love each other "as I [Jesus] have loved you." When this kind of love operates within the fellowship of the church, it is a visible and completely convincing proof of the reality of Jesus, which even a blinded world cannot help but recognize. Love within the body, Jesus' kind of love, is the divinely ordained means by which "all men will know" that we are His disciples.

Strikingly, love has even more benefits and impact. In looking through the Bible's teaching on spiritual gifts — those workings of the Holy Spirit through believers by which He builds His body toward maturity — we find that in each biblical context great emphasis is placed on the relational climate in which

46

spiritual gifts operate. Spiritual gifts are not related in Scripture to *office* — with the gift of teaching restricted to Sunday school, and so on. Instead, spiritual gifts and their operation are related to *involvement in people's lives.* When the love relationship between believers exists and is being expressed in a mutual ministry of concern and encouragement, then the Holy Spirit works His miracles of grace, and uses each believer in his unique way, making contribution through the human personality in the way His sovereignty has chosen to enrich the lives of others in the body.

It is not surprising, then, to discover that a second distinguishing mark of evangelical renewal is love: the growth of "family feeling" in the church. It is the growing realization that each person is loved and accepted, and the growing joy of reaching out to build one another in the Lord. In each of the three churches visited, many speak of the sense of love and family feeling that pervades the fellowship. As they speak, it's clear that however family feeling is attained, it is an essential element of what these churches have become.

Our Heritage

At Our Heritage, the family emphasis is seen in every activity. The church has essentially two gatherings: one on Sunday of the whole congregation, the other a weekday meeting of believers in the twenty-some "little churches."

In each setting great stress is placed on sharing. Sunday sees the two-hour morning service involve initial sharing through worship — elements of which are spontaneously suggested by the congregation — then, following the preaching ministry, continued sharing, exhortation, discussion, and prayer and prayer requests. The "little churches," too, feature close relationships, developing gradually and kept in focus by the prayer and Bible study emphasis.

About the unity and love that mark the fellowship, Pastor Bob Girard comments, "The unity of the church is to be built on the basis of love, not some secondary thing. It needs to be released from whatever superficial things hold churches together. In other words, the church is supposed to be personal. It's supposed to really care, and there is no way a church can care except personally. I mean getting together for something that is really personal.

"The church has to get personal and stop being afraid to get personal."

Of barriers to personal relationships, Audrey Girard suggests, "I think progress — progress in basic caring for what goes on inside other people and how you can help them find their way to life in the Lord — is thwarted and slowed down by the fact that they've got to be so busy."

How do you help a congregation move from busy-ness to business? Bob tells a little about the thinking that led to the changes at Our Heritage: "Your goal is a congregation that really loves each other and ministers to each other's needs. Well, that outlines your steps a little. You've got to find some ways, some places where this can happen and begin to encourage it to happen. You have to talk about it happening, and help it happen where you can. There may be some places in some churches in which you can't be personal. But maybe there is a Sunday school class where you can be. Or maybe it's a midweek service. Maybe it's the board meetings. Maybe it's just the relationships among staff members in a church that has a multiple staff.

"In every church, if a guy is willing, there are some steps that can be taken. It can be almost obvious. Here's our goal: We want to learn to love each other, to learn to minister to each other. Well, there has to be some place that is giving the chance for this to start. For us, as with a lot of other churches, there just wasn't any place where this could happen. That's why we started the 'little churches.'"

Mariners

Small groups play a role in the life of Mariners Church too. Talk with the members of the church, and as they share what's happening in their lives, they mention over and over again the relationships with others they have come to know and love in smaller groups. Lou, whom we will meet in Chapter Eleven, comes out plainly: "If I had to choose, and I'm glad I don't, I'd take our Tuesday night group over Sunday."

Martha, a gal who lived most of her life in the fast-paced, slick, and superficial world of California advertising, tells about her group with tears in her eyes. "We don't want to lose the family feeling. We actually meet each other's needs; we actually meet financial and spiritual needs. Food has been taken to someone who is in trouble. Money has been taken; some was given to me.

"People find out someone's need. I had a need. I imagine the only way they could find out was because Lawana found me in tears one day. It was a real need.

"Another woman called me last week almost on the verge of hysteria. A lovely person, she had to have some serious surgery and it was possibly cancer. Now, in this case the need isn't money at this time, or food, but she certainly does need a lot of loving care, because most of her friends are non-Christians.

"One of the women was running into trouble trying to feed three kids, and they hadn't had meat for a couple of weeks. So the guys in our group went to their freezers and took out stacks of meat, and Lawana carried it down there. How they found out, I don't know. God lets us know. God can let us know each other's needs and help us care."

One board member sees the importance of the groups this way: "Although God provides forgiveness, sometimes we don't really feel as if He does. We need to see it reflected off other Christians. I noticed that this is what was happening in our body life and our home Bible studies; we were beginning to see and feel that God really accepted us, because the people all around us really accepted us. For the first time in my Christian experience I began to feel I could do my own thing, differently than I had been allowed to do it before in a church. I think this is particularly important in people who have come from non-Christian backgrounds. They need to feel this warmth and acceptance from the Lord, and the way they get this is from other Christians first."

Certainly this is the way Carolyn, a new Christian, experiences the church. "The warmth in this church is incredible among the body. I go to the Tuesday women's prayer group, and that has meant more to me than anything. Well, anything except for the Lord and Joe's preaching the Word. But the women's prayer group gives you the feeling of being part of the body. I don't have any problem sharing at all. There's truly a tremendous amount of love. If anybody had told me about it a year ago, I wouldn't have believed it."

Sometimes we're suspicious of such sharing groups. I asked one of the men if sharing doesn't generate talk or an overemphasis on sins. The response: "I've never heard it happen. I've heard people question whether it would happen or not. We had an incident last summer at Mount Hermon. On the last evening they had a sharing session, and a gal who was an unwed mother got up and said she had a terrible sin to share with the group. We figured that, well, here it comes — for the first time somebody's going to let go something that shouldn't be shared with a group. But it didn't happen. It was in good taste, nothing anybody could object to at all. I've never heard anything that would be objectionable: just honest problems and not in vivid detail. It's not necessary to go into detail. Just sharing where you're hurting."

What happens when people share where they are hurting? "God seems to pair people when they share something like that. Invariably there's somebody there who has gone down that same road before. Or at least someone who knows someone and can share what's happened in his life and can respond with encouragement."

Joan, a woman at Our Heritage, sums up what people at both churches seemed to be saying about their groups: "We care for each other and minister to each other, and I think that's what God intended. No one stands up to preach a sermon. We're not theologians, and I realize that we should have more knowledge of the Bible probably. But we really do care about each other, we do take care of each other's needs, and we do minister to each other. And as the Bible says, we laugh together, we cry together, and we really share each other's burdens. I think that's vitally important."

Putting it all together, Jack says, "It's a great opportunity here with Mariners. With the teaching that we've been getting, and the counseling we've been getting, and the fellowship we've been getting. It's a completely new experience for us. It's been exciting for us!"

Trinity

When Gib Martin insists "We're not building our church around small groups or Bible studies, and we don't even want that kind of language spread around here," you get an initial jolt. Then, talking with him, you begin to see that the *opportunity to be personal* doesn't have to be provided by groups at all! In fact, Trinity has developed an even more intense "family feeling" using different means.

Where in the life of Trinity do the people have the opportunity to be personal, develop love and express it, and minister to each other? Everywhere!

Mary talks about what happens when one of the ministry groups at Trinity gets together in a board meeting to plan for the coming month: "Well, there are about seven of us, and we meet at my house usually. We have coffee — except once I forgot. We usually visit a bit, just about things that are happening in the families of the people on the board, and we have quite a good time in prayer for one another, and for people having trouble in the church. And then we go through the practical details of planning showers and meetings, and you know."

About the ministry of the Women's Fellowship which Mary led for a year, she says, "It's a ministry of encouragement. The thing that the Lord has been showing me is that you can't encourage people until you know them. So we try to have a monthly meeting with quite a bit of time for just getting to know one another. That's the main emphasis as I see it: getting to know one another."

This is the same theme reflected by Gary, head of the Sky Club. "I look at board meetings as more than just discussing business. It's a time we can fellowship together, learn a bit about each of us, and what God is doing in our lives, and any problems. It's as much a time of fellowship as it is of business."

This dimension of dynamic fellowship developed and expressed in all the "business" meetings is something Gib is aware of — and has taken the lead in encouraging.

Virginia suggests another source of the intense family feeling that exists at Trinity. "My concept of discipling isn't so much a structured thing. It is the discipling that is going on in the church now on the one-to-one basis. The Lord actually gives you someone who is drawn to you or it's a mutual thing and you pray together, as with the girls [in the study center or the Grapevine] we take under our wings. We pray with them, they're free to come to our home at any time, and we try to make them feel free if they have any. kind of problems. A substitute mother and father are available to them."

It would be unfair to write of Trinity and not mention something that Gib speaks of often, with enthusiasm: the widows. He views as one of the great strengths of Trinity its giving widows a proper, biblical role in the life of the church. These women not only serve with the Grapevine Auxiliary, but are keys in the prayer ministry of the church. They enrich the warmth of the Grapevine ministry by their involvement, and increasingly they are taking on the task of one-on-one ministry to younger women in the church, teaching them to love their husbands and children.

The Sunday evening "Schools of Christian Living," held three times a year for eight to twelve weeks, also emphasize interaction and involvement during 2½-hour sessions. The "love" emphasis in the Sunday morning services further heightens awareness that the body is a family — a family that loves and cares for its own, and for all the hurt and broken whom God allows it to reach out to and touch.

Family

The deep, personal commitment of the members of these bodies to one another is not the whole story of their renewal. But the reality of their love for one another is, with other factors, a necessary condition!

Spiritual health in the body of Christ is never present apart from love. And love is never present except where people come to know and care for one another personally, as unique and precious individuals. The personal dimension is a universal characteristic of renewal.

It's important to realize that the personal dimension can come into the life of the church and be expressed in a variety of ways and settings. Small groups. Informal, sharing congregational services. One-on-one relationships. Board and committee meetings. Counseling. Classes. Whenever believers get together, they can and should take time to care for each other — and then, united in spirit and love, they can perform the tasks to which they are called.

It's also important to realize that the personal tone of the church is set by the leaders. It is set by the pastor, who lives as a real person with the people (not a cardboard figure of a holy man). It is set by the elders, who build unity between themselves and thus are able to mirror the kind of love God wants to create in the whole church. It is only as the climate of love is established and grows that a local body becomes a fellowship prepared by God to bring forth beauty.

7 « The Word and evangelism

These three churches reflect still another necessary dimension of churches in evangelical renewal. Each church has a commitment to know — and to do — the Word of God.

Jesus, in the high-priestly prayer of John 17, called on the Father to sanctify believers through the truth which His Word is. The dynamic, cleansing, transforming process of sanctification can only take place as the Word of God purges us of distorted perspectives on life, and as obedience to the Word releases us to experience the true freedom of the sons of God.

Gib Martin puts it this way: "The thing that has helped me is John 8. The freedom. I sense in every heart a demand to be free. So freedom is what I've looked for — freedom from my lusts, freedom from my passions, and freedom from my bigotry. And freedom from my ignorance. Freedom from my dogmatism. Freedom from man, from being the pawn of some man. Freedom from religion. Freedom from hate. And then freedom to love. Freedom to be. Bringing every dimension of freedom I can possibly bring is one thing I work on in the minds of men. The Word of God is the way there. If you continue in the Word, you will be free."

Rather than finding commitment to the Word of God restricting, as some seem to think it would be, the men and women of the three churches have found in wholehearted commitment to Scripture's revelation of God's will a distinctive and joyful freedom.

Bob Girard sees much of his ministry as helping people realize the headship of Jesus Christ. "He's not only the head of the church, right now, today — He's the head of each of us and wants to communicate His leadership, His lordship, which He does through the Word. This is also done in a very existential way, to people who are truly related to Him and related to one another in Him."

About the Bible in the life of Our Heritage teens, Ron Rogers says, "This may sound trite, but the kids see it as a blue-print for life. They have their Bibles with them constantly be-cause it's important to them. This is God, who is really com-municating to them. The most important thing to them is not knowledge of this Word, but knowledge of the Person of the Word. The Bible is the truth about the Truth."

At Mariners the people speak often of "the truth about the Truth" and its role in their lives. One woman says this:

"This church is completely straight from the Bible. There's no confusion. I never listen to a sermon and feel it's Joe's opinion, or Joe's dad's opinion, or somebody's opinion who taught in a class at Dallas Seminary. Joe makes no mistakes that this is God whom he is quoting, and you never feel Joe is saying it. He seems to be very careful, and if he does say 'in my opin-ion,' he clarifies it.

"Joe in his sermons has taught me something I had a hard time learning. This is the Bible, and this is what it says, and this is what God says. If you don't like it, Martha, that's too bad. That's your problem. And you know, that's the way it is.

"Now I love it. We have to have something we can depend on, and even if we don't agree with it at first or wish we could change it, there's a satisfaction knowing that this cannot be changed. This is the way God is — and this is what we really all want, isn't it?"

It would be wrong to form an impression from this that the ministry of the Word is primarily informational and doctrinal at Mariners. The same woman continues: "For me the sermons have made the Bible alive, a living Book. Joe preached the Jonah series, and in that showed me things about Jonah that I am doing today in my life. So the Bible comes alive, and I can say I know Jonah almost because I know myself, and I can see why Jonah did the things he did. In David, or in Ephesians, you can see yourself."

Focusing on the preaching ministry and the weekday Bible

studies, another suggests, "The Bible really is the basis of this church."

A couple — new believers — tell of the role Scripture has played in their own lives, and how their relationships have changed. "What has really changed," says Bobbie, "is the attitudes. We haven't seen a tremendous amount of complete changes in our marriage, but new attitudes on the part of both of us, the desire to see the other person happy, the desire to please the other. A new commitment would be a good way to phrase it. Both of us have a real hunger for the Word, desire to study the Bible, and a deeper desire for prayer. After we do all the reading, we find prayer is really making the changes."

Evangelism

At each of the three churches you meet new believers — men, women, and children who have recently come to Jesus and are excited about the difference He is making in their lives. Yet the evangelism that is going on is of a quiet kind. There are few organized "campaigns," few agencies that push people out to witness or are designed to draw the non-Christian into the church.

Gib Martin notes, "We have been very low key in what is traditionally called evangelism. I feel that the Great Commission says to disciple, and it does not say to evangelize. I think evangelism is an extension of a mature disciple. A mature disciple does evangelize. So I've worked on the principle that evangelism is the outgrowth of maturity, not working to have babies lying around a nursery and to fill up pews."

Has this approach worked? The number of people being won to Christ by members of these three churches says Yes! At Mariners, Dave tells about the quiet approach his wife Linda has seen develop: "She and Gail got together late last year and started a Bible study at home. They studied the Gospel of John first, and they've made it a Bible study and sharing time. Monday mornings they hire a baby-sitter from UCI, and she moves the car out of the garage, and there is an average of eighteen kids out in the garage. That was a test for me. I'd come home Monday night wondering what had been destroyed in the yard that morning! But it's been worthwhile too. There have been at least four girls come to know the Lord; in one family the wife became a Christian as a result of this, and now they're having tremendous problems. If it hadn't been for the Lord . . . ! I just have total faith now that their problems are going to work out, and I believe the husband is close to coming to the Lord.

"Two other families bring results directly from this Bible study. Dave and his wife became Christians in February, and they've done a 180-degree turn. It's phenomenal. The same thing happened to Jim and Georgia. They've known the Lord for only six months, and she found the Lord at that Monday morning Bible study."

A number of the believers who attend Mariners spearhead a local evangelistic Christian Leadership Week in March. They arrange for speakers, meet in the local clubs, have meetings in the morning for businessmen and in the evening for families. But like the rest of evangelism at Mariners, it is done by the men and women of the church without, as Joe puts it, "the brand name *Mariners* on it."

When I challenged Bob Girard with the question of whether Our Heritage is an "unevangelistic" church, his response too was, "Not at all! But we don't push people to share. It just comes out."

Bob tells one incident about Frank, a professional entertainer and pianist who came to Christ about three years ago.

"Frank and his wife went down to park at a swap place," Bob says, "I think it was a Sunday, which would blow some people's minds. A *swap* is a place where you take your junk down to sell, and they were down there parked in a stall next to another guy. They started talking, and he kept asking more questions, he was so hungry. He would go take care of a customer and rush right back for more. They shared with him about the Lord for three or four hours, but he wasn't sure he wanted to respond. He told them he'd keep in touch. Well, this man lives in Tucson, and next week he called them up to tell them he had given his life to the Lord. But he said, 'Now, what am I going to do with my wife!' He thought she would be really turned off. During the next two weeks he won his wife to the Lord.

"Now he's down in Tucson. Our church will never see the numbers, but there was real joy in the congregation when Frank shared this, and you could see Christ alive in Frank. We still communicate with this new brother and we take care of each other."

Often "numbers" are deceiving as far as evangelism is concerned. Ron Rogers from Our Heritage tells of a hitchhiker he picked up: "The night before he had asked the Lord, 'Lord, give me somebody I can fellowship with, or I'm going to die.' And the Lord said to me, 'Pick up this guy.' And now he's moving toward full-time Christian work.

"One of the younger men in the group now feels definitely called to minister in the Lutheran church. One of the others is not full-time professionally, but he is full-time period; he's working in Greeley, Colorado. Another has a full-time ministry while he's going to school in a church here in Scottsdale, and he is having a tremendous ministry. His Bible study has three times as many as mine does. It used to bother me I really got jealous. Here was this guy — I taught him everything he knew and that kind of thing — and in numbers he's beaten me by leaps and bounds. Then he in turn has an action group of men he's discipling, and so I'm really pleased by that because I see things begin to mushroom."

One by one, the people won and discipled in the nurturing ministries of these churches are beginning to reproduce themselves. With maturity *has* come evangelism. A quiet, personal, one-to-one kind that may not show up in statistics, but has a multiplying impact on the church as a whole and is constantly bringing individuals and families to the Savior.

I tried to get exact numbers from the leaders of these three churches. It was difficult, because they don't keep statistics. But it is clear that *at least* five hundred people this past year have come to know Jesus through the ministry of the men and women of Our Heritage, Mariners, and Trinity. Possibly the true count is twice that figure!

Why aren't statistics kept? Because in each church there is a focus on people, not programs or numbers. There is a deep and growing personal concern for individuals that reaches out to share the love of Christ with brother and potential brother alike. There is the conviction that as believers grow toward maturity in Christ, *God* will give the increase.

This quiet approach to evangelism, along with servant leadership, family feeling, and commitment to the Word of God, seems to mark most renewal churches. It is not that winning people to Jesus is unimportant; it seems rather that the focus is placed, as Gib Martin says, "on maturing believers." As believers mature, they *do* reproduce. Where there is maturity, there seems little need for pushing people into a witness that may seem unreal because Christ has not been formed sufficiently in the one who testifies of Him. Instead there seems to be with maturity a boldly written "letter about Christ delivered . . . and written, not with pen and ink but with the Spirit of the living God, engraved not on stone, but on human hearts" (2 Cor. 3:3).

Part II « THE PRODUCT

In which we look at the results of church renewal and at criteria for evaluating church effectiveness.

8 « How do we evaluate churches?

There are, of course, the obvious criteria: conversions, size, giving. Certainly these criteria are indicators of something happening in a local body. And certainly, too, these are results we should desire.

God is concerned about bringing people to Jesus: we can hardly be unconcerned! The old excuse for stagnancy, that "we're concerned about quality rather than quantity," has to be rejected and recognized for what it is. Where there *is* quality, where there *is* a dynamic work of the Holy Spirit in and among God's people, there will be evangelism.

It is, however, difficult to equate "growth" and evangelistic effectiveness. Today believers are scattered through their communities. Those they contact and win to Christ — if the evangelism of the church is truly an "every member" kind of thing — may never come to the evangelists' church! This is seen at Our Heritage, for example, where evangelism is personal rather than focused through organized church efforts. Of the many who come to Christ through the witness of believers there, the great majority never settle into the Scottsdale church. Matching memberships and conversions is not really valid. Only when the evangelistic efforts are focused on getting people into the church (as in a bus ministry) can the two be equated.

Giving, though a meaningful indicator, of God's working among a people, is not a sufficient standard in itself. Surely, as Matthew 6:21 says, "Where your treasure is, there will your heart be also." Heart and treasure. No wonder giving, the growth of giving the missionary budget, and the rest are taken as reflecting the health and dedication of a local church.

63

But the question is more complicated than this. For example, giving in the thousands of dollars may mean less in a church in an upper-middle-class neighborhood than the giving of hundreds in a poverty area. Again, one body may stress "storehouse giving" in which all giving is channeled through the local church; in another like Our Heritage, as a recent study showed, giving may be evenly divided (51 percent through the church, 49 percent directly to people in need, for missionary support). Figures are important, yes, but they need interpretation!

There are other issues as well. In the New Testament we learn that money was given to Paul and other missionaries for their support. But the emphasis is on the meeting of human need! Throughout the Old Testament as well, concern for the poor is constantly stressed. James's illustration of blessing the brother in need rather than feeding and clothing him help to bring home to us the fact that in the early church . . . and possibly in God's eyes . . . people have priority over program. Thus it is not just "money given" that should be counted in our evaluation. We also need to explore carefully the priorities expressed in our giving and see if these are in harmony with God's priorities.

Incomplete

These factors make me dissatisfied with the usual indicators we point to as evidence of church health. Yes, large numbers can be impressive. But at best such data is incomplete. At worst it can even be deceptive! There is the example of the Illinois church which suddenly tripled attendance and was written up in the denominational paper — in an article which disclosed that the growth came through the relocation of a seminary nearby!

There are other, even more significant indicators. The Scripture itself focuses our attention on indicators that can't be treated statistically, yet are known by participants when they are present. In fact, they parallel characteristics we noted in the lives of the three churches in this book.

Interaction is an indicator. How much do believers in the local body share with each other? Is there the "bearing of one another's burdens" that the Bible exhorts? Do we encourage one another? Exhort? Teach? Is the body *ministering* or *passive*?

Involvement in the lives of others both within and outside the church is an indicator. Are the believers who make up the local body experiencing significant relationships with other persons? Is concern for needs — physical, social, and economic as well as spiritual — evidenced in their actions and interests?

It is important to note that in citing these indicators we are essentially shifting from *general criteria of organizational health* to *in-person indicators of individual growth.* Strikingly, criteria like size, number of conversions and amount of giving all focus on measuring the product of the whole. Thus, what is being measured is not what is happening in the lives of individuals, except in the most indirect way. Rather, what is being measured is what the organization has produced!

In essence, renewal says that the truly significant indicator of church health is the *growth in Christ* the local body is facilitating in the believer. Criteria which pose questions about what is happening in the individual are the crucial ones! Thus, in looking at "conversion" figures we also want to ask whether these numbers reflect a growing ability of the believers of the church to share Christ, or if they reflect an ability of the organization to program responses to invitations. This assumes not only that those won to Christ by friends are more likely to be *discipled* than those won through some mass effort; it also assumes that God is deeply concerned about the nurture and growth of believers into discipleship. Therefore, evidences of a discipled life are critical in evaluating church effectiveness.

The discipled life

This whole emphasis is rooted deeply in Scripture. The Great Commission charged the first believers to go out to "make disciples." Conversion to Christ was seen as the *beginning,* not the *end,* of Christ's mission in the lives of men.

Thus, the fruit of the Holy Spirit's presence in the lives of believers, which the Bible emphasizes, is not reproduction but "love, joy, peace, patience, kindness," and the rest (Gal. 5:22, 23). God seems to focus His attention, and ours, on a ministry *within believers* through which their personalities are progressively transformed.

This concept of transformation is basic to our understanding of Christian faith and life. We see it reflected in many ways in Scripture. Jesus hints at it in Matthew 5:45, in which He tells His disciples to love their enemies "so that you may be sons of your heavenly Father. For he makes his sun rise upon evil men as well as good, and he sends his rain upon honest and dishonest men alike." The disciples' love is not to be modeled on the love pagans show, responding to those who love them. Rather, the disciples' love is to be patterned after God's own love: they are to "be perfect as your Heavenly Father is perfect" (Matt. 5:48).

The expectation that believers are to *be* like God is stated boldly by Peter. "Don't let your character be molded by the desires of your ignorant days, but be holy in every part of your lives, for the one who has called you is himself holy" (1 Peter 1:14, 15). The words are jolting and shocking, for clearly this demand is beyond our capabilities! But Peter continues — and explains, "For you are not just mortals now but sons of God; the live, permanent Word of the living God has given you his own indestructible heredity" (1 Peter 1:23).

We can be like God, for as His sons we have His life in us. Christ's own life, implanted in our personalities at conversion, is the source of all beauty. Because of the gift of life Jesus has given us, we *can* and *are to* become like Him. Indeed, we are told in Romans that God actually chose us "to bear the family likeness of his Son, that he might be the eldest of a family of many brothers" (8:29). It is our destiny to be like him.

This destiny will be fulfilled only at Christ's coming, when we are fully like Him. Of this John says, "Here and now, my dear friends, we *are* God's children. We don't know what we shall become in the future. We only know that when he appears we shall be like him, for we shall see him as he is" (1 John 3:2). Yet at the same time it is true that *"here and now"* we are God's children. *The transforming process, the transformation of our sin-warped personalities toward the beauty of Jesus Christ, begins now!* Paul says, "All of us who are Christians . . . reflect like mirrors the glory of the Lord. We are transformed in ever-increasing splendour into his own image, and this is the work of the Lord who is the Spirit" (2 Cor. 3:18).

Strikingly, the ministries which God performs in this world through His body, the church, are all related to the shaping of

Jesus' likeness in the believer! The love that reaches out to touch another person and draw him to the Savior is rooted in this likeness. Paul, speaking of the ministry of reconciliation, calls Christlike love "the very spring of our actions" (2 Cor. 5:14). As Jesus' likeness is progressively formed in us, we are freed to love as He loves. The virtues which free us to live lovingly with others — "love, joy, peace, patience, kindness, generosity, fidelity, tolerance and self-control" — are fruit produced by the Holy Spirit in human lives, crowding out the "hatred, strife, jealousy, bad temper, rivalry, and envy" (Gal. 5:20, 21) which are our natural heritage. Transformation is *first concern* of God for His church, for upon it all other spiritual ministries hinge.

Evaluation?

When we think, then, of evaluating the effectiveness of the local body of believers, we must realize that *in-person* changes are the critical indicators of church health and effectiveness. When in the local body believers are growing in Christ, personalities are being transformed, Christ's love is being extended to brothers and sisters and outsiders alike, when there is a growing responsiveness to the Word, *then* and only then can we begin even to think of the church as "successful."

As we saw in Chapter Seven, this emphasis is *not* a denial of evangelism. Instead it provides the only firm basis on which evangelism — if that evangelism has in view the total discipling process as well as initial conversion — can rest. But the numerical indicators we are so quick to fasten on are *not* and dare not be accepted as the primary criteria by which to evaluate the life of a local church, if our concept of the church is in any way rooted in the Scripture's revelation.

It is also difficult to accept the numerical indicators as accurate representations of a progressive change or growth in church health. For instance, until a few years ago Mariners was not a "growing" church. Then suddenly within a three-year-span, membership tripled! Was the church a failure until growth came? Or was growth a result of the longer process of building a basis of church health? (A basis which at least in part explains the dramatic impact of the local body on its community *without any of those programs* which the Big Churches rely on to bring in people.) It is personal evangelism which, with the preaching of Joe Aldrich, lies at the heart of Mariners' growth. And it is always personal evangelism that will develop as a part of the life style of that local church in which transformation is the focal concern.

Perhaps, then, it is best to think of evaluation in terms of seeing God at work in the lives of believers — what happens when the Spirit of God touches individuals' lives and in the context of the body produces in them Jesus' own unique beauty.

And so let's look at illustrations of what we can expect to see in the lives of men and women whom Christ is transforming through the ministry of His body. The examples chosen are *not* isolated or unique in the membership of the three churches. They are instead the pattern, not of the life of every participant, but of the lives of many. I firmly believe that the best possible indicator of church health is to discover God at work in just these ways in the lives of significant numbers of members of the local body.

When you read their stories, perhaps you will find this transformation particularly significant, too.

9 « Suzie: a whole new way to live

I've known Suzie for over a year, through Our Heritage Church in Scottsdale, Arizona, which we both attend. She and John have shared their ups and downs with our church family and encouraged us all as God has answered many prayers. We talked with Suzie in a public housing apartment God had just provided for the family, and we saw something of the beauty of trust.

I've been a Christian for about three and one-half years now. I became a Christian at Our Heritage Church, led to the Lord by some kids at the ASU [Arizona State] campus. One day when my life was in a real muddle, a girl friend upstairs gave me a Four Spiritual Laws booklet. I thought well, that's nice, and I merely put it aside and didn't think too much more about it. But the Lord was working in me, showing me some areas in my life that I couldn't do anything about. He gave me a desire to go to church, which is really strange, because I wasn't raised in a church and had been in very few churches. So I told this girl that I was going to go to church with her, and she picked me up the next Sunday. That Sunday I got up and thought of all kinds of reasons why I couldn't go to church, and when she got there I backed out.

It took three Sundays before I finally got up nerve to go to church. The girl attended Our Heritage, and through the whole sermon it seemed as if that man was really talking to me. He was a fantastic speaker. When I had been in other churches, I didn't understand what was going on and went away feeling like I hadn't been there. But this was a different

69

thing. The third Sunday I was there, we had a Communion service. I'd never known what Communion was, and through that Communion service the Lord spoke to my heart and I received Christ.

I went through some pretty traumatic things right after that. The Lord moved John and me far, far away, into west Phoenix. We spent about a year away from the church and away from any kind of fellowship. In that year the Lord taught me how to pray by making me so miserable that one day I just sat down and said, "Lord, I don't know what to do." I prayed and I learned to pray.

Until I became a Christian, I did not want another child. I wanted nothing more to do with motherhood. I'd had all I could take. But He blessed us with another child. God became very real to me that year, and one of the ways was our daughter. Until I was six and a half months pregnant, the baby seemed dead. She had no life, she had no movement, she had no heartbeat; the doctors couldn't find anything at all. Finally, lying in bed one night, I told the Lord I didn't know how to pray and I didn't know if I had a right to pray. But if it were His will, I would like to know if the baby's dead or alive.

About three or four days later, it was my birthday and we went to a movie — and the baby began to kick and to move in an extraordinary way, so I knew she was alive. God had given her life, you know, right then. I carried her for the full nine months, and she was born. She had a few problems when she was born, and had to spend some time in the hospital. I had to trust Him for that, too, so she's a true gift from God — one of the things we can look at from day to day and can thank Him for.

The strange thing, after I had her, is that God seemed to give me a gift of evangelism. But at that point I didn't even know what that was. I had a Jewish roommate in the hospital when Jennifer was born. I didn't know there was a difference between a Jewish person and me — we're all just people. So I spent half a night telling this girl all the things Christ had done for me, having no idea how I must have been offending her, just sharing my own life with her. Since then God has used me in other lives, and He's moved us all over Phoenix. We've lived in Scottsdale, in Tempe, in west Phoenix, and in south Phoenix, and in each place where we've been, God has allowed us to affect lives, and He's used us to bring people to the Lord. He's moved people in with us to counsel with, to help to know Him better, and it's a fantastic life.

It's not a very stable life so far as the world counts stability. My husband has been in numerous jobs since we've become Christians. Previously he was always at the same job, but since he's been a Christian God has moved him around from job to job.

A basic thing was that we seldom had enough food, and I'm the kind of person who, before God began showing me things, could throw out leftovers without a second thought. God began working with me in this matter. I would much rather have gone to the store and bought things already made, or gone out to dinner, than stand over a stove and cook. One of the first things He showed me is that I have to shop on His budget. I had to live on a budget (which is totally impossible, with discipline and details of life that bore me to death). I had to be able to shop within that budget, because there have been weeks when we had two dollars for a week's groceries. We've had to live on that, and we went through some tough times in order to do that.

One week we had ten dollars' worth of groceries, and I had just bought them and put them in the refrigerator. We were living in south Phoenix at this time. We had a dear Christian sister, who doesn't have a husband and lives all by herself, and she has four little children. She called on the phone to say she didn't have any food. I had just put all that food away, and God said to me, "I want you to give her all that food." I thought, "Lord, if I do that I won't have anything to eat. Still, this was what He wanted me to do, and I said Okay. My husband came home, and I said, "I gave all our food away." He looked at me puzzled and I said, "This is what God wants us to do." John said, "Okay, you go ahead and do it, if that's what God wants you to do."

So we gave away all our food. And God miraculously provided. I was on a diet, then, and I was anemic. Doctor bills had been a big thing, too, and at this time, being anemic, I had to eat a lot of liver and other foods with high iron content. We came back from giving those groceries away (I don't know if it was the same night or the next night), but there was a check for ten dollars in the mail. We just couldn't believe it. We went down and we bought another ten dollars' worth of groceries for us. So He taught me by that how blessed it truly is to give to people who need it, and know that He still takes care of you. We've never forgotten that lesson. We've never forgotten how to go ahead and not worry about our own needs.

When Jennifer was born, we had a big thing about clothes because we've never lived where we've had a lot of money. I don't think I ever consciously said to the Lord, "Lord, you're going to have to provide for her," and yet He has, and this child has never so much as had a pair of shoes bought for her since she's been born. She's never had a diaper bought for her by us. Everything she wears, everything she has, has been given to her.

The people in the church have added greatly to my growth, and our needs being met. Sometimes even when needs weren't expressed, they still were met. God has introduced us to different segments of our church, people in our church, one at a time. It seems as if no one is there to meet the same need, and there's never an identical occasion when I call the same person twice. It's always a brand new relationship or a brand new need being met or a brand new ministry.

It's fantastic! We've had medical bills that were just overwhelming. I've been in the hospital, I can't even tell you how many times, in the last three years. Once I went in for mononucleosis and this resulted in gall bladder surgery seventeen days later, with a $2,000 doctor bill, our hospital bill, and a $500 surgeon's bill — and just all kinds of things. Still, they let me go home with nothing paid on the bills, which is highly unusual.

During that time in the hospital, I led five people to the Lord. In those seventeen days I had three different roommates on three different floors, and five people came to receive the Lord while I was there. My stepmother and my stepfather were separated at the time, and God put their marriage back together while I was there. Each time I've been in the hospital, it's been almost the same thing — except the last time I was in isolation, so I am not sure what God's purpose for that was.

It's a miraculous way to live, and I've fought with Satan about this a lot, and with the flesh, because the flesh says you're living off other people and you're taking advantage of other people. But God has a whole new way of life, and this is what it is for us. We've often said, "God, why are you doing this to us?" We can look at other people in our church or around us who haven't nearly gone through the trials we have, and we say, "God, why us?" Then we just look around and say, "Well, we're witnesses to how life can be lived trusting God day by day."

10 « Dave: the world turned upside down

I met Dave at Mariners Church in Newport Beach. He's a relaxed, friendly, thirty-year-old, the kind of person it's comfortable to have around your home or your church, the kind to whom success came too easily — and turned to failure. In Dave, beauty is a total transformation of values which has withstood both financial disaster and a record sixteen million dollars in sales for Penn Mutual this past year.

I grew up in Los Angeles, moved to Newport Beach when I was fifteen years old, went to high school here, college in Los Angeles at Occidental, came back here, and started in the life insurance business in 1963. I married in '64. We were semi-active in a large church in the area between '64 and '66 and then dropped out of church all together. I was involved in a business venture at the time that coincided with our dropping out of church, and I got my life screwed up morally and financially.

I had accepted the Lord when I was thirteen but had not much knowledge. We were exposed to Mariners Church in 1968, through Bill Beck and Bob Milam. We went almost every Sunday, but still I wasn't involved emotionally with the Lord, or even intellectually.

In May 1968, when the stock was at the height, I was a socially acceptable schizophrenic. Have you ever seen that Disney cartoon where the mild-mannered suburbanite businessman walks out of the house in the morning and gets behind the wheel and turns into a fiery-eyed demon? Well, I was the same way. Only, I turned into a fiery-eyed demon when I boarded an airplane and headed off to wherever I was going. I lived the role of a businessman on the company expense account. I drove a Lincoln with a telephone in it, and the only telephone call I ever got was from my brother-in-law, calling me to see if the phone really worked.

I was living high at twenty-seven years old. Not only that, I was the coffee tender at Mariners Church at that time. You know, I drove up in my big Lincoln and pulled the coffee pot out, and I was the only guy who made coffee for everyone after church service, then on Monday morning I would be on an airplane flying to St. Louis and swinging in some night club that night. That's schizophrenic, and you eventually crack up.

You know, if I hadn't met the Lord I'd have wound up like a lot of other guys. That's what's exciting to me. It's meaningful to share that with businessmen when you know so well that's what they're going through. They're trying to be this real cool guy over here, but they would surely like to be a plain, simple family man, and it just tears them apart.

In late 1969 financial disaster struck this particular corporation in which I held stock, and it collapsed. I owed the bank a lot of money, so I went back into the life insurance business, still not paying much attention to spiritual things at all. In the fall of '70 I was visited by some Mormon missionaries, and they laid out a plan of salvation and a plan for life on their flannel graphs in our home six weeks in a row. It sounded pretty good to me, because I had so many pressures at the time, and it was a way to lay everything out. But Linda wouldn't have anything to do with it. Finally Bill Beck and Milam heard that I almost became a Mormon, and they got to me and showed me the way through the Scriptures a little.

I rededicated my life to the Lord at that time, and it was about a year later that I began to gain some knowledge, get my role straightened out, and began to talk things over properly with my wife. I can look back and think that the troubles I had between 1966 and 1970 were just getting me ready for the commitment I made in 1971. Even though things got a little bit worse financially after I accepted the Lord in '71, it has been absolutely one miracle after another. The Lord has totally changed my life and my attitude and my business opportunities.

This year has been the most dynamic year of my life in terms of my relationship with the Lord, my wife, and my business. It so overwhelms me that I think about it day by day.

Of course, I think that's what the Lord's trying to tell me anyway. But I had to learn to live with this financial burden day by day or I would've gone "stir-crazy," Christian or not. I'm up to the point now at which He's relieved that pressure, and I'm so overwhelmed by the way it's been relieved that I almost fear I'm going to get messed up again. But I know that's not going to happen and I just pray that the Lord will really make me aware.

I've never been the kind of person who says "Okay, Holy Spirit, lead me." I like to say, "Okay, Lord, this is what I think You want me to do now. If it's not, You show me the obvious signs and I'll ask You about it every day." That's the way I'm living my life right now in all areas. Linda and I pray every day that the opportunities we have will be used for a good ministry.

But let me talk about my personal spiritual life first. I've become more honest with the Lord about my problems. I know He knows about them anyway, but I've been able to talk about them with Him and be specific. From the teaching we have here at Mariners, I'm very specific in my prayers. If I've committed a sin, I specifically talk about it, whereas before I would skirt the issue; and so now I feel closer to the Lord. It's the first time in my spiritual pilgrimage that I'm not afraid of the Lord's returning.

Let me explain what I mean. I always knew that a Christian is supposed to look forward to the Lord's coming back. But you think, man, I've got it going so good that if He comes back now, it's going to blow the whole deal! This is the first time in my life that I've become fond of the Lord. I can't really say that I love the Lord as much as I love my wife, because I haven't gotten to that emotional level yet. But I can see it coming now. I can see that the relationship is good. And it doesn't take away any other relationships. It only improves them.

I've been involved in CBMC [Christian Business Men's Committee] and Operation Timothy, and that's forced me in a practical way to better understand my beliefs and to be able to communicate them to someone who is either a new Christian or not a Christian at all.

The Lord has helped me to start to depend on Him daily as far as marriage is concerned. This is the first year Linda and I have prayed together. This has been a phenomenal experience. Fortunately we haven't gotten stuck on the ritual of it, so we can be quite open with it. There were some things that I did back in '68 and '69, when I was involved in this other corporation, that I was finally able to confess to her, and that really bridged the gap and made it possible to talk about other intimate things we could never talk about before. I found out that she questioned whether she really loved me or not just as recently as two years ago. This was hard for me to accept. Now she says openly that she really does.

We like to use our home for a ministry. We're having two attorneys over Friday night whom I've worked with considerably this year. I don't think either of them is a Christian, but one did all the estate planning for an insurance client of mine who became a Christian the same time I came back to the Lord. This attorney comes into the client's office, and the first thing he says to the attorney is "Dave and I believe that Christ was the Son of God." This attorney is sitting there, well, thinking maybe, What have I got myself into? The second interview was dynamic because it involved a daughter whom he wanted to treat a little differently in his will and who is a very emotional part of this man's life. So the attorney was dealing with that, and the client got so moved he said, "Well, why don't we close this in prayer." Then when he signed the will (my wife and his wife and the attorney were all there), Mr. Larson closed in prayer again. So they're coming over for dinner.

I told Linda last night, "Let's just kind of cool it on the spiritual things for Joe's benefit, because we've had the tendency to say, 'Okay, the stage is set, and we've got to work on just being ourselves, and not avoiding it, but being careful.'"

Dave's sixteen-million-dollar sales record has given him opportunity to speak at several sales conferences.

I happen to be in a business position and in an industry that's really ego-centered, in which they love super-salesmen. There are very few people I can share with concerning the way some of my sales have materialized this year. When I stand up before a life-insurance audience to talk, they're going to think, "This guy has a magic key to success," and they will want to find out what it is. I have opportunities this year — one in front of a pretty big audience — to share my faith, and what's really exciting to me is that I'm going to have people's attention. Rather than tell how to sell life insurance, I'm going to share the experiences I've gone through since I've been in the business. Of course, the dominant thing I learned is the spiritual side of life, and I try to really spread the gospel in whatever way I can.

Being a businessman and in sales, I see many people all week long. I believe I can relate to the fact that most men are living lives of quiet desperation and need the strength that Christ can give them.

11 « Lou and Barbara: through the needle's eye

I met Lou and Barbara at Mariners Church. They came in together — Lou, a vigorous fifty with the face and physique of a man who knows what hard, physical work is like; Barbara, a delicate blond, warm and quiet. You'd never pick Lou out of a crowd as a man who built a $500 backyard investment into eight multimillion dollar businesses. But just a little conversation with them and you discover beauty: the beauty that comes when God brings a rich man through the needle's eye, and turns drive into devotion. And the beauty that emerges when God takes defeat, and works through weakness.

Barbara. I came to the Lord through my daughter. My only "Christian" education had been Catholic school. Neither of my parents were Christians in the sense that we think of it today, and they never practiced any faith, so I had many hangups with guilt in that regard. I'm the kind of person who has fear and guilt problems, who gets frustrated and angry. Some neighbors took our kids to church every Sunday, which was fine. Boy, that took the burden of guilt off me, and I could sleep late, and they were getting some Christian exposure anyway. As our daughter came to her teens, she rededicated herself to the Lord, and we saw this change taking place in her. It was dramatic, and it was such a marvelous thing to observe that we wondered, "Why is it happening?"

I did receive the Lord finally in a Billy Graham Crusade, and then I didn't do anything about it. I accepted Him as Savior and not as Lord, so the Lord kept on dealing with me.

I had turned totally into an introvert, and I couldn't talk to people. I got to where I couldn't even express myself to my family, and that hurt. I spent most of my time under the covers, hiding, staying up late at night, hoping the next day wouldn't come. Still, the Lord kept bringing more and more Christian young people into our lives. Finally all these different emotions — watching these young people, having the feelings of jealousy at their growth, and knowledge of my own guilt — well, finally I threw in the towel and took some sleeping pills. I had come to the bottom, so I think the Lord guided Lou to wake me up; I'd left the light on (I often fall asleep reading), and he usually goes over and turns it off. But he touched me for some reason, and I don't remember a thing —

Lou. She was actually writing, not a suicide note, but a note saying that she just —

Barbara. I couldn't find the Lord.

Lou. She was searching and just couldn't find the way to respond and just scribbled off into nothing, so I knew something was wrong.

Barbara. I guess it was a pretty destructive evening for my family. I looked like a rag doll, and Lou said he never thought I could weigh that much, so he went to wake up my daughter, and of course they had a terrifying night. Lou took me to a hospital here locally, and I went into group therapy. There were a lot of good staff people. They were well trained and had an excellent psychiatrist, whom we're now trying to bring to the Lord.

I was still getting desperate, so my daughter said, "Why don't you call Mariners?" So I called, and Nayda was here at the time. I was really bawling. I was in bad shape and wasn't getting any answers. I was told to make the choices, but who gives you the strength to? Who gives you the will to? This is where psychiatry stops and there has to be something else.

Nayda was just fantastic to me over the phone, and Joe wasn't there. I was so frustrated, I was going to hang up, but she kept me on the phone and told me she would try to reach him. Then he tried for days to get in touch with me, because at the hospital they wouldn't give him my name or tell him where I was or anything. All he had was my name, and all we had was a public phone we could dial out on. Anyway, Joe finally reached me and came over, and I just blubbered the whole bit to him.

(Pastor) Joe. I felt totally helpless.

Barbara. No, he wasn't. We never had a good chance to talk, but I couldn't believe that a perfect stranger would come and give so much time and bring me a book to read. I'd never met the Aldriches, and Ruthe, Joe's wife, was truly friendly and open. But the one thing Joe said that I hung on to for a long time was, "If the Lord wants to use you, you can't commit suicide. There's no way — I don't care whether you drive over a cliff or what you do. If the Lord wants to use you and has a future for you, there's no way you're going to check out." And you know, he went back and shared Moses with me, and how he was a recluse too and the Lord really had to drag him by his heels out of the desert. Remember that?

Joe. It was a turning point, because Barbara then shared with me the fact that if I'm good enough for the Lord to use me, I must be important. Prior to that she didn't feel she was important at all. This was the first spark of really feeling some value.

Barbara. Joe said, "Well, the Lord brings us all to our knees in different ways." He said Jesus had to bring you to your knees, to get totally helpless, and that was a concept I'd never heard before. I thought it was still a "work your way to heaven" bit, and as far as I was concerned — particularly with my Catholic background and then a divorce and being responsible for five children — I figured I'd blown it a long time ago. I don't really fully understand.

There was another gentleman who was in the hospital when I was, who had been a lay preacher, and I think the Lord brought the two of us together. He had lost the Lord, and we encouraged each other. He looked like the strong one, and he wasn't, and we had a little Christian group going that made it different.

Joe. Then she's evangelizing the whole mental ward over at the hospital, holding services in her room, and all of a sudden she becomes the chaplain and everyone's coming to share their problems with her.

Lou. It's been going ever since. One thing she learned there and told to me — and I saw it happen — was that in the mental ward she went into group therapy and automatically the barriers came down. They shared in group therapy where they hurt, and because they were total strangers, they were willing to risk. She'd never had that experience, and that's why we immediately took the home Bible study that we have. It's amazing that everyone shares and risks things, and by doing that you get so close to people. The minute you share a weakness, everybody's serious. Of course, in the Bible study group we not only expose our hurts, but we also share what to do about them.

Barbara. We focus on God, so when you come to the group, you have the assurance that a person has the same principles you're working with. For example, in the hospital we weren't expected to love one another; there just wasn't any love involved. Not God's love anyway. It just dawned on me that this year we have learned to love one another in this whole new way, of perfect acceptance. Now we're capable to the point at which we can admonish each other in love, and that's real growth. Now I see what Christ's love is about. It's not going out and saying I love everybody. If anything, it's seeing Christ's love through each one of these people.

Sometimes we worry about going back to our old friends, and how to act. In the summer I had asked the Lord to let me rest on the whole thing, because it had taken me years to get this in me. Now I need a cork to quit talking. But we were worried about, well, here we are in swinging Newport Beach, and if you come on strong about the Lord in your local club, yacht club, or tennis club, people start giving you a very wide berth. You scare them, sometimes, when you first accept the Lord. This summer we had a moonlight sail which usually ends up as a drunken ball. We sail until everyone falls off the boat. Some way or another we ended up at this one fellow's house. We drank that night, but it wasn't anything I needed to relax me any more; I drank because I felt like it, and I didn't want them to think I couldn't love these people, because they're made in the image of God. I felt a little risky, that I might get sucked back in, but Lou was there. We didn't get loaded, but we spent the whole time talking about the Lord until five o'clock in the morning, and we finished with our host. He could not understand my saying, "I'm so happy that I can wake up every morning and say I'm a total failure. I don't have to live up to anybody's expectations."

Lou. Joe, we have the biggest drunkard halfway to where he's listening to your tapes. He's willing to listen. He says, "Man, if God can change your life like He has . . ."

Joe. It might be interesting for Larry to hear how you came to know the Lord in the midst of all this. It was all part of the crisis and experience.

Lou. Well, as Barbara said, we're totally opposite. She has been very shy, withdrawn; a problem with self-image. The only time she would talk like this was when she had had a few drinks. It took quite a few drinks to get her to open up. Now she's open like this without ever having a drink. People just can't understand how all of a sudden . . .

Barbara. There's a different person in there.

Lou. But I'm just the opposite. I'm always outward and filled with a lot of drive and confidence. I was raised in a Presbyterian church back in Milwaukee, and I got turned off because it was cold and hypocritical. I just never heard the message and didn't see it in anyone's life.

After the war I finished school and started in business. When you start a new business, you always push to get the business to a certain size. I'd do that, and then I would set another goal each time. I didn't realize until after becoming a Christian the reason why it is that the greater the goal, the greater the yuckiness. I was just running in the opposite direction from Christ. I never really got away because the emptiness was bigger. I didn't realize that the greater the ego, the greater the emptiness. I think the majority of businessmen or professional men are just on an ego trip. *I* was — there's no doubt about it. Yet to feed the ego, you have to do bigger and better things, and you know there's no satisfaction once you reach a goal.

Barbara. You remember how the Bible says, "It's harder for a rich man to come to Christ than it is for a camel to go through the eye of a needle" (cf. Matt. 19:24). Joe really nailed Lou one day. I could tell. I was afraid to look at him the whole time.

Lou. I was sitting in church. This was on August 20 — a year ago August — and the Lord had been working for about two years. Prior to that our daughter turned sixteen, and this was when the whole family really saw a change in her life. The change was a daily change: I mean, she just was like the flip side of a record.

She was a very quiet kind of wallflower, and all of a sudden she started bubbling over. We thought it would wear off, but it just stayed, and she's still that way. So we all wondered, "What's the matter with Kathy? What's wrong?" She told us not only that she had become a Christian, but that she had Christ in her life daily. This was my first real experience of understanding that the Christian life is not something that happens only on Sundays, but a daily, living thing.

Kathy walked with the Lord, daily depending on Him. It was almost scary, because she had so much faith; yet we saw her grow and grow. It permeated the whole family. One day, sometime later, she asked me if I were a Christian. I said, "Well, sure I am." I thought I was, because I was raised in a Presbyterian church. I was baptized in the Presbyterian church and I thought that made me a Christian. I think the greatest travesty nowadays is that churches are filled with people who think they're Christians, and they're not getting the fruits and the joy of Christianity, so they don't realize what it's all about —

Barbara. They're not told how to love one another. I think that's the whole thing in a nutshell.

Lou. So when Kathy asked if I were a Christian, I said, "Well, sure." That's when I started questioning and wondering what it was all about. After accepting the Lord here at Mariners on August 20, I saw the growth in Barbara, who was below zero to start, and it was obvious to everyone. She became stronger and stronger. In the past, I was always involved. Now it was happening without me, so when we had the opportunity, we started going to this Bible study. I think one of the shocking things to all of us came when we went down on a trip to Texas —

Joe. I took them both to a conference.

Lou. They asked me to share my testimony, which I had not done, and it put me into a state of shock. I relieved the emotions of it step-by-step as it happened. Later the Wallaces, whom we had just barely met, heard that Barbara's father had fallen and broken his hip and his wrist, and was in a hospital in Denver. We heard about it while we were at the conference. It seemed very serious, because they couldn't operate on him

— they were afraid he was going into pneumonia and shock, so we were really worried. That evening before the Wallaces went back to their motel room, they said, "Do you want to pray about it?" So here were total strangers, who didn't know Barbara's father and just barely knew us, yet they were praying for him.

If we had to make a choice — which I'm glad we don't have to — between going to our Tuesday night Bible study or to church on Sunday, we'd put our priority on the Tuesday night Bible study. I sincerely believe that the warmth we get in our Bible study permeates the church, rather than the body permeating the Bible study. You get open with people only in small groups; once you have shared a need in a small group and have found acceptance, you're willing to step out and share in the body life here in the church. You test the water, and if you don't feel rejected then, it gives you more confidence and you share more openly.

Barbara. You don't understand God's love or His acceptance apart from the way He manifests it through other people, through other Christians. He tells us this, but if you don't come into contact with love, you know nothing about it. As I said, this is the thing I realize now. I know how much being an empty vessel and letting His love show through really means, because I've seen examples of it in people.

Lou. There is one thing I find helpful in a marital relationship. In the past, I would talk about things that interested me, and Barbara was centered on something that interested her, and they never seemed to tolerate each other. One thing leads to another, and you're arguing. But now we both talk about the Lord. When this happens, your whole lives start coming together, because you know the minute you're focusing away from self and away from other people, you're focusing on talking about the Lord. Barbara radiates when she talks about the Lord. She just lights up like a light bulb.

I've lived my whole life with planning — a schedule for the next year, planning everything — and I was always disappointed because plans never worked out. Now, taking each day at a time, it's really exciting. Things happen, and they just keep happening at a faster pace. I think the turning point throughout is that the Christian life is a daily, exciting experience. It's not a salvation at the end of the line. It's not a Sunday. It's not a social affair. It's an exciting way to live each day. That's the thing that turned us on. It's foreign until you experience it and see it. It doesn't matter how many times someone tells you something, I believe the thing happens when you see it in person.

Barbara. I believe the Lord has shown me that I needn't worry about getting shaped into a Christian mold. I was fearful of this. I believe this is a major problem with so many people of my nature: we're afraid to allow the Lord full control because He's going to tell us something we don't want to hear. I found out that the things I worry about, the Lord doesn't. I don't have to worry about taking things out of my life. I don't have to worry about taking out bad habits. The Lord is bringing so many new things into my life that it's where He wants my focus.

Lou. We all start out feeling we have to shape up. When you realize you don't have to shape up, you simply must have faith and read the Word, the Holy Spirit will shape you up.

Barbara. But you have to have a group in which you can honestly bounce off your ideas and your questions and your ideas, because you have to have help reading the Word. I got into Romans; Romans almost killed me. But, the Wallaces are in our Bible study, are mature Christians, and can express their failings and say, "Okay, now how do I resolve this?" Thus the Lord shows me how I can let Him do His will in my life.

Lou. I think this is the overriding concept that has brought about more change in our lives than anything else. When you share a weakness of yourself, a failure, to these people you love, it becomes a strength. I've had trouble relating to my teenage son. The minute I went in and said I'm sorry for doing something and admitted and asked for his forgiveness, he changed like that, and he and I now are growing closer. When you share a weakness, it becomes a strength. It happens over and over again.

Barbara. He gives us answers through our brothers and sisters in Christ.

Lou. If you had known Barbara a year and a half ago, you wouldn't even recognize her today, because she's completely transformed from an introvert and quiet person to an outgoing person, a complete switch. We changed roles, you see. She was the introvert and very quiet; I was the domineering, outward, strong person. She has now become strong through her Christian growth, and now I realized that all these worldly things aren't worth a teakettle. Now I'm learning real values, so in that way we're coming together in the real world.

12 « Ivan, Susan, and Pat: the unhooked

At Trinity Church in Seattle I sat facing Ivan, Pat, and Susan in the Grapevine, a house turned into a center for community ministry. Each of these young people came to Christ out of the drug culture. Each was growing spiritually; each revealed something of the beauty that comes when chains are broken and life is linked at every turn to the Lord.

Ivan. Maybe I ought to start at the beginning and tell briefly what Christ has done in my life. I became a Christian on July 2, 1972, and I was in the county jail in Seattle, Washington, cell C-3. I was in jail for second degree assault and armed robbery, and I was a drug addict or a user for about 6 years. I had a grandma who loved me and prayed for me for twenty-one years, and I accepted Jesus Christ on that July 2. I had lived at the Grapevine for about a month and a half before I went to jail; after I was released from jail September 25, I moved into the Grapevine again and started to go to school.

The Grapevine had a great ministry to me. A year ago I received my first report card from school, and I got a zero point zero grade average. I asked God to change my life, because I had a desire to get an education and do something that would count for Jesus Christ, because I really loved Him. So the Lord changed that part of my life. He's really given me a victory when it comes to grades. The first quarter I received a 3.29, and then a 3.77 in the next quarter. I have shared this to show you the miracle that has taken place in my life.

I am working now at Caldwell Health Center. Last year at the training center we had a series on spiritual gifts, and God pointed out to me that my spiritual gift was exhortation. I prayed all summer while I was working at the camp that God would give me a ministry which would improve my gift and be a job at the same time. He gave me a job at Caldwell Health Center working with older people and meeting their needs and sharing Christ with them — and encouraging them, because those people need encouraging.

I worked there for a week. One man there (his name is Jim) has multiple sclerosis. One day I was taking him into the whirlpool. I'd shared the Lord with him, and I asked him for some reason if he was ready to accept Christ into his heart. He said yes, he was, so we prayed right there, and he accepted Jesus Christ. I've seen some beautiful things happen in people's lives while working there, and it's been a fantastic experience for me.

In my own growth I think that the Grapevine Shelter was a key. We learned a lot about discipline and about setting goals for ourselves. Mark was the director, and he was a great one for that. I learned about goals through his example and through the examples of men here who love the Lord and are following Him. Maybe something I learned is studying the Word and praying. These were something that kind of worked into my life. If I had a sincere desire to grow, I would have to get into God's Word to be changed, and I saw that God could change me through His Word.

My desire right now is to get deeper into the Word and to know the truth so the Lord can set me free — and also set people around me free because they've seen the truth in me. Also, I remember how, when I was in that drug world, I hated people who had gray hair. But these people in the body of Christ made it so real to me; people like El McFall and Eva Graham loved me for who I was, even though I was unlovable. And that changed my life.

What's the situation today? I struggle, I do struggle. In fact, I was at a friend's house today, and I realized there's still temptation; yet I know I have a Lord who is watching out for me. I love Him so much that I don't want to hurt the love I have for Him. But there's still a desire, and I think anyone who says that those things just leave would be lying. In my personal experience with Christ, the old man is passing away and I am becoming new, but the old man is still there.

Susan. Before I came here, I didn't have drug problems. But I wasn't a Christian, just a miserable person. I was living with a man I then broke up with, and I didn't have anyplace to go. My mom has attended Trinity Church for about ten years, and she said I could come here. So I came here chiefly because I had nowhere else to go. When I first came, I simply wanted to get a job and save some money and move out. I told my parents not to talk to me about God. They tried to make me go to Sunday school and church and Bible study; but I would rebel and say you can't make me, and would they please quit doing this. They'd make me go anyway, and I hated it. To live with them I had to go.

I went, and I acted miserably, and people asked, "What's wrong?" And I said, "I'm not a Christian and I hate it and I don't want to be here." But Pat came when I'd been here a couple of months. We started liking each other, neither of us being a Christian. Immediately we planned to move out and live with each other. It got back to Mark and Gib and everybody in the church, I guess, so they talked to us about not doing it because I'd get hurt and all that. But we intended to do it anyway.

What the people in the church did was not to force me not to go away with Pat, but to pray for us. They just prayed and loved us and, well, what happened is, they prayed for me to become a Christian. I tried to fight it at first. I told God, "Leave me alone — I don't want you."

I finally gave in, and when I gave in, my whole life changed. I was like a different person overnight, my countenance and everything changed, and I was happy for the first time. I had purpose; church had a new meaning. Instead of going to church and hating it, everything sounded as if I'd never heard it before. For the first time I heard the verses and the hymns, and for the first time I was able to love the people in the church, and they loved me. They mean a lot to me now. Pat and I were married about a year later.

Right now I guess being married is a struggle. In the Bible God warns you that you're going to have real problems, and I can see why He does. It is difficult for a husband and wife to please each other as the Bible tells us, but it seems worth it.

My need now is to grow in studying the Bible. I'm very undisciplined. It's not the Bible that I don't like — it's the study-ing. As in school: I dropped out of high school because I hated to study and read. Now I need to discipline my life in studying so I can combat Satan and the world and know the Scriptures in order to tell other people about it.

A girl at my work, Kathy, was at the study center. She works here during the day. She is truly together spiritually, and I try to meet with her every week. We haven't started a Bible study, but she wants to deal with me and pray with me; that helps, because it gets a little lonely just being a wife without much company.

Pat. I became a Christian about a year ago August, and at first I decided to stop doing everything — stop taking drugs and drinking and smoking and swearing — and try to be a perfect person. At the end of five days I couldn't stand it any more, and I left here and went out with some friends and got high and started drinking. What I learned from that is that God is the One who changes me and I can't do it myself. That's the thing I try to do all the time: to get up and start running and trying to do what's right, and all of a sudden I find out God isn't with me, and I fall flat on my face. Then I have to spend some time on my knees and get my heart right with God again and start listening to what He has to say.

My parents are Catholic, and I spent my first four years of school in a Catholic school. After that I still had to go to church with my family every Sunday. As soon as I turned seventeen, I joined the army and immediately stopped going to church. I rebelled against the idea of being forced to do something I didn't want to do.

One time I got mixed up with a shooting and a bank robbery. The people I was with shot a police officer, and I was the only one who got away. I went to Canada and into a church. I was alone, and I went there and promised God I would never do it again. I'm not sure exactly what I said, but I know that at that time I was sincerely seeking God.

Ivan and I grew up together, and we were co-partners in many bad things through the drug years. He came here first, and I was living up in Capital Hill. I was depressed and lonely, and I was shooting speed at the time.

I was talking to Ivan one day and shared with him my feelings. He told me to talk to Mark and Gib. So I made an appointment and came here to talk to them. They accepted me. I promised to submit to their authority for a certain period of time. Some other people were almost certain I wouldn't last a week before leaving, because my heart was truly rebellious. Nevertheless, I stuck with it and about a month and a half later accepted the Lord. But I fought against everything here; whatever they tried to do I rebelled against.

The only thing I couldn't cope with was the love they showed me. That is the one thing which finally broke me. There was an honest, genuine love, something I'd been looking for all my life. I can't say that my parents didn't love me, but I never *felt* loved by them. I've seen love here. Even after all the terrible things I said to the people, the threats I made, and all the things I did here, they still loved me and tried to show me the right things to do and help me grow up.

Their program isn't a general kind of program for everybody. They try to build a program to suit a particular person. It's an individual kind of thing, and it involves studying and working in the yard. For the first two weeks I was here, I wasn't allowed to make any phone calls or see my old friends. I was completely cut off from the outside world. Later on, Susan was here. We met and began a relationship.

About two weeks ago I decided to set goals and make plans for the future and help Susan develop the things she really wants to do with her life. I was working with prayer at the time. I read in Second Chronicles that we're supposed to humble ourselves and pray and seek His face and He will hear us. I was starting to do these things when all of a sudden everything went haywire. I fell back about twenty steps, and Susan and I started arguing and not getting along.

I came here today to talk to Mark alone for a few minutes and confess my sins and spend some time in prayer with him. It's difficult for me, too: I want to have a close personal relationship with God, and I want that to be a reality. It's difficult to have that in your early years of growing with the Lord. But I want Him to be as real as you are to me or as my wife is. I want Him to be that close to me and know He's there.

Part III « THE PASTORS

In which we look at the Sunday
ministry of the Word and again see
differences between the churches . . .
yet within the framework of a
shared commitment.

13 « The role of the pastor

The pastor — his person and his preaching — is critical in the life of any church. Today we give pastoral leadership perhaps too central a role in church life. Yet it remains a fact that in today's church, whether traditional or renewal, the pastor is the key man. To some extent, the local body is shaped and molded by his personality and his emphasis. His ministry of the Word will be reflected in the way the congregation studies the Scriptures individually and in smaller groups. If he is doctrinaire, doctrine is likely to be the emphasis of their study. If he is personal, emphasizing application, they are likely to build on the example he sets.

To a highly significant degree, the churches described in this book reflect the personalities of the pastors. Our Heritage is a revolutionary church: Bob Girard is a revolutionary person, a man with the strength to act on his convictions. Mariners is a church with freedom and sensitivity to individuals: Joe Aldrich is a warm, personal, and positive man. Joe's preaching reflects this warm and applicational approach. Trinity Church is a church in mission: Gib Martin is a man convinced of God's call to serve. Gib's teaching and messages and his personal example help to channel the energies of the believer-priests into fully committed ministry.

This relationship between the men God calls to a local body and the shape the Holy Spirit gives the body itself is a natural one. In the infinite complexity of God's own personality and His plan, there is room for infinite diversity. Each local body can and should expect to take on its own distinctive character and emphases. In this process, believers are very likely to be guided by the man God has called to be with them. "Those things, which you have both learned, and received, and heard, and seen in me," Paul said to the Philippians, "do" (4:9 KJV). They were to model themselves on the example of the apostle. No wonder the spiritual leaders of the church — who Peter says are to be "examples of Christian living" rather than dictators over the flock — will be imitated in the life of the body (1 Peter 5:3).

In a strong way, the pastor then stands as a model of what the people of the church are becoming. His strengths and weaknesses are reproduced in the congregation. His emphases are visible in the shape the local body takes. No wonder we see in the preaching of the pastors of these three churches clear indications of each minister's own emphases — and the emphases already noted as characterizing the bodies.

As we look at the three sermons that constitute this section of the book, we readily see that these are not "homiletical gems." Probably none would find its way into a collection of famous sermons. But each one *is* typical of the man and the thrust of his ministry. Each one also reflects a total commitment to the Word of God as the fully sufficient and completely reliable *present* Word to God's people.

14 « Bob Girard

It is characteristic of Bob Girard's preaching ministry that he focuses on issues which affect the life of the local body as a church. In this he may neglect at times the more personal needs, the focus on truths that build up individuals, or guidance for their personal struggles.

But at Our Heritage Bob ministers in many ways besides his preaching. In the open sharing time which marks each service, Bob takes the lead in openness and in disclosing both the struggles and victories in living for Jesus. Also, the Little Churches, in which 70 percent of the congregation regularly take part, are well equipped to provide the more personal "growth" truth and emphasis.

The message selected for this chapter is typical of Bob's in many ways. It first of all grew out of a particular need of the local body. Our Heritage is not a charismatic church; yet its services are open, with freedom for sharing and expression given to all who come. Though not charismatic, the church takes no strong "anti" stand on such phenomena as speaking in tongues. The underlying attitude is one of accepting as brothers all who know Jesus, and one of rejecting *all* tendencies to create divisions between members of Christ's body on whatever grounds.

Thus, when a visitor did "speak in tongues" one Sunday morning, the issue was discussed by the church leadership. Certainly one was not going to speak *against* brothers and their convictions, since the charismatic expression is not clearly condemned in the Word. Also, a number of brothers and sisters in the local congregation do speak in tongues,

97

although privately and not in the church services. How should the local body be guided to respond? What guidelines could be given for members which did not hinge on the "rightness" or "wrongness" of this experience, which affirmed unity, and which gave a basis for maintaining unity, yet put the whole question in some kind of perspective?

The solution was a series of sermons, and first of these, "Up With the Son," is reproduced here (in edited form). In it Bob guides the church to see the absolute priority of Jesus, and thus to avoid the danger of seeking in some additional relationship with the Holy Spirit something beyond or better than knowing Jesus.

The printed words cannot capture the dynamic way Bob Girard presents his material. Nevertheless, they do reflect his consistent emphasis on Scripture, his practice of searching the whole Word and integrating many references into his messages, and his way of meeting issues facing the church with a study of God's Word to find the *basic answers* (rather than superficial ones) to guide the body in response.

Up With the Son

There is one and true living God. He is perfect in sovereignty, justice, righteousness, love, eternal life, omniscience — which means he knows everything, omnipotence — which means He has all power, omnipresence — which means He's everywhere at once. He is eternal and perfect in these things. In that perfect unity of the one and only God there are three persons, God the Father, God the Son, and God the Holy Spirit. These three are one — one God. Now that's a heavy concept. One God with three co-eternal, co-equal persons, who are one in essence. That means that all three persons are of the same substance. They make up the same being. They are mentioned together as persons in Matthew 28:19; John 14:26; 2 Corinthians 13:13, 14; and 1 Peter 1:2.

It's not really possible to worship, serve, and relate to the three persons separately, as though they were three Gods. They are not three Gods, but one God. Whenever we worship, serve, or relate to one person of the Trinity, we are at the same time in touch with the other two, because they are one. Whenever we worship Jesus the Son, we are also in touch with the Father, we are also praying to and in touch with the Son and the Holy Spirit. Whenever you obey the Son, you are obeying God. Whenever you grieve the Spirit, you grieve God. Whenever you receive, listen to, follow, trust, or reject one person of the Trinity, you receive, listen to, follow, trust, or reject the only true God. Here it is in Matthew 10:40: "He who receives you," Jesus says to His followers, "receives Me, and he who receives Me receives Him who sent Me." To receive the Son is to receive the Father. And in John 12:44 Jesus says, "He who believes in Me does not believe in Me, but in Him who sent Me." By believing in the Second Person of the Trinity, we are automatically believing in the First Person of the Trinity.

The titles given to the Holy Spirit declare the same truth. Romans 8, for instance. In that single chapter, the Holy Spirit is called "the Spirit of life in Christ Jesus" (v. 2), "the Spirit of God" (v. 9), "the Spirit of Christ" (v. 9), "the Spirit of Him who raised Jesus from the dead" (v. 11), and "the Spirit Himself" (v. 16). Further evidence of their inseparability is in John 7:37-39 and Acts 2:38, in which faith in Christ is declared the only requisite to receiving the gift of the Holy Spirit and the rivers of living water that He is within us. You can't receive the Spirit without receiving Jesus Christ. And when you do receive Jesus Christ, you at the same time receive the Holy Spirit, according to those passages.

In the order of the Trinity, the eternal council of the holy Trinity, an order is established. An order is established among the persons of the Godhead. First of all there is an order of authority. In 1 Corinthians 11:3, God is the head of Christ, and in John 12:49 Jesus says, "I did not speak on My own initiative, but the Father Himself who sent Me has given Me commandment what to say, and what to speak." And again in John 14:31 He says, "As the Father gave Me commandment, even so I do," and in John 6:38, "I have come down from Heaven, not to do My own will, but the will of Him who sent Me." Even though Jesus can say, "I and the Father are one" (John 10:30), yet in the decision of God in eternity, the Son willingly places Himself under the headship of the Father. How does the Holy Spirit fit into the order of authority in the Trinity? In John

14:16 Jesus says, "I will ask the Father, and He will give you another Helper, that He may be with you forever."

The Father has authority over the Spirit in addition to having authority over the Son. And the Father commissions the Spirit to do His work among men. "The Holy Spirit, whom the Father will send in My name," says Jesus, "He will teach you all things and will bring to your remembrance all that I say to you" [John 14:26]. Then in John 16:7 Jesus says of the Spirit, "I will send Him to you." Jesus has authority over the Spirit as well. And in verse 13, "He will not speak on His own initiative, but whatever He hears, He will speak." From what source will the Spirit hear what He speaks? John 16:14: "He shall take of Mine," says Jesus, "and shall disclose it to you." Then, lest the order of authority be forgotten, Jesus adds in verse 15, "All things that the Father has are Mine; therefore I said, that He [the Spirit] takes of Mine, and disclose it to you."

Draw it all together now. The Father, the Son, and the Holy Spirit are essentially one. The divine, self-determined authority lying within the Trinity is (a) the Son submits to the authority of the Father and receives His commandments from the Father, which He willingly obeys; (b) the Spirit also submits to the authority of the Father and receives His commission from the Father, which He willingly carries out; and (c) now that Jesus is ascended to the Father, He has been given authority to send the Holy Spirit (John 16:7) to continue and complete the Son's work in the world; (d) everything that the Son has, He has received from the Father; (e) everything that the Spirit has was received from the Father and the Son.

The Spirit willingly submits to the Father and to the Son. The three persons in the Trinity have willingly placed themselves in submission to each other and are by divine choice utterly dependent on one another. None of them acts independently of the other two. All possess absolute power unto perfection, but have chosen to submit to one another in absolute unity and harmony of purpose. There is an established line of authority, and it is a part of the harmony of the Trinity.

There is, in God's great eternal plan, an order of glorification — a clearly designated order of glorification. It follows the order of authority. From the beginning, even before the beginning of time, God planned that He would receive glory and honor and praise and celebration from His creation through one particular channel. The worship and glorification of God centers on one person of the Trinity. John 17:1: "Father, the hour has come; glorify Thy Son that the Son may glorify Thee." Verse 4: "I glorified Thee on the earth, having accomplished the work which Thou hast given Me to do." Verse 5: "Now, glorify Thou Me together with Thyself, Father, with the glory which I ever had with Thee before the world was." John 13:31, 32: "Now is the Son of Man glorified, and God is glorified in [through, by means of] Him [the Son]; . . . God will also glorify Him in Himself." John 14:13: "And whatever you ask in My name," says Jesus, "that will I do, that the Father may be glorified in the Son."

The plan of God is to receive His glory and His praise and His worship and honor and celebration through the Son. When the Son gets glory and praise, the Father who sent Him is getting the same kind of glory and praise through Him, because to touch the Son is to touch the Father.

This is very important. When we gather together, we gather around the Son. We come together in the Son's name (Matt. 18:20). We pray in the Son's name (John 14:13). We do our work in the Son's name (Col. 3:17). When the Holy Spirit does His work, when He is poured upon us, baptizes us, or leads us, or empowers us, or teaches us, or chastens us, or gifts us, or uses us, the focal point of the Holy Spirit's ministry is exactly the same. In John 16:14 Jesus, speaking of the Holy Spirit, describes the whole thrust of the Spirit's work in these terms: "He shall glorify Me; for He shall take of Mine, and shall disclose it to you."

Don't try to slice them apart! "He will teach you all things," says Jesus [in John 14:26], "and bring to your remembrance all that I said to you." The Holy Spirit does not seek to glorify Himself, and there is no evidence in the New Testament that the church is to worship or exalt or glorify the Spirit. Wherever the Spirit is working, wherever He's moving, Jesus Christ — not the Spirit — is in everybody's thoughts. Jesus is receiving the primary glory, and the Father is being glorified in the Son. The focus of everyone's attention is on Jesus when the Spirit is at work and is truly controlling the situation.

Even in Acts, which some have called the "Acts of the Holy

Spirit," we find the Spirit continually camouflaging Himself, persistently pushing Jesus forward to the point at which men and women are believing in Jesus and envisioning Jesus and are being healed by Jesus and set free in Jesus and working in the power of Jesus, receiving confirmation of the reality of the living Jesus Christ, proclaiming Jesus all over the world. Luke starts out in chapter one, verse one of the Book of Acts by indicating that he intends in Acts to continue to tell what Jesus continued to do after His ascension to the Father. Every page exalts Jesus. The Holy Spirit is there working all the way through it, you can't miss it, but Jesus is the One put forward at all times. When they went out, they proclaimed Jesus. The Holy Spirit does His work without being proclaimed!

That is the divine plan. The whole business of God's getting the honor due Him revolves around the Son. The Spirit glorifies the Son because when the Son receives glorification, the Father is being glorified. The Father is glorified in the Son, and that's why the whole work of the Spirit among us is to bring glory to the Son. Praise and honor and notice and celebration and obedience and exaltation focus on the Son, the Lord Jesus Christ. The Holy Spirit is purposely in the background, not so distinctly revealed to us as the Son. The Spirit's work is not to call attention to Himself, but to call attention to Jesus.

This gets out of focus when our concern is for experiences and gifts and something spectacular. We forget that Jesus, not the Spirit, is the One around whom we gather and in whose name we live. The Spirit is grieved whenever that happens. His work is hindered, and the world misses the point. It is important to understand that our relationship is not with one person of the Trinity, and then another. There are not, in the Christian life, three separate relationships — one with the Father, a second with the Son, and a third with the Spirit. There are not even two separate relationships, one with Jesus and the second with the Spirit. There is one God, not three. We Christians are not tritheistic, but monotheistic — one God. The Bible is not tritheistic, but monotheistic — one God.

When you relate to one person of the Trinity, you relate to the others as well. If you know the Son, you know the Father and the Spirit. If you know Jesus, you know the Spirit. When you are in the Spirit, you are in Jesus. There are not two levels

of spiritual life — one with Jesus for salvation, and a higher
with the Spirit for power. *The highest place to which a man
can attain is to be in Christ.* Everything God has planned for
the believer is available to him through Christ. We are, says
Colossians 2:10, complete in Christ, complete in Jesus. When
we have Christ, we have all things (1 Cor. 3:22, 23).

The Spirit who indwells us is the Spirit of Jesus Christ,
specifically designated so. The Jesus of history, the Christ of
Scripture, the Christ of the Gospels, He is the Spirit. The Christ
of the Epistles, He is the Spirit. The Christ of the Revelation,
He is the Spirit. The Spirit is He. The Spirit who indwells us
is the Spirit of Jesus. To know Jesus Christ, to have received
Him and His Spirit crying within us "Abba, Father," is the
greatest and the highest opportunity known to man. No experience is greater than that of new life. Only the mind of man
could conclude that there is a greater experience.

I know that people are quite innocent as they do it. I think
it is something we need to back off from: Only the mind of man
could conclude that there is a greater experience than Jesus' new
life. There is no experience beyond knowing Jesus Christ. There
are many wonderful experiences *in* Jesus Christ. There is un-
folding a more and more glorious experience of Jesus Christ,
more of His power, more of His gifts, more of His grace, His
love, more of Him to experience. But keep it straight. Jesus
Christ is all-sufficient. If we truly know *Him,* He is our all-suf-
ficiency. There is nothing beyond that or better than that or
greater than that, because that's everything God ever intended
to give us!

If, after you are born again, you do come into some blazing
new light, or experience a spiritual breakthrough, or experience
special fillings of the Spirit, or experience a miracle, or you grow
sometimes by leaps instead of baby steps, or you begin using
new gifts, or you discover new joy or new faith or a new sense
of reality of God, keep it straight! Understand that all of this is
available to you only through Jesus and for His glory and only
because you know Him.

It is not that you have come into something higher than knowing Christ. There is nothing higher! You know Him better, perhaps, but you don't know anything better than knowing Him.
It's not that now you have something better than the new birth,

or that now you have the Spirit whereas before you only had Christ; rather, to have Christ is to have all that God is intending to give us in this life and in eternity.

Everything truly good in our lives is because of Him and because we know Him. The Holy Spirit does nothing that does not happen as a result of knowing Christ, and the Holy Spirit does nothing but what is intended to lift up Jesus Christ to glory and praise and honor. Experiences and growth subsequent to regeneration are not separate or better. They result from your being in Christ, and thus in the Spirit, the moment you truly receive Jesus Christ by faith. In Christ, life will get better and better as we move by the Spirit from glory to glory.

The response I'm hoping for and praying for is that the congregation of Our Heritage may continually keep Jesus Christ in the center of our meetings, our worship, our work, and all of church life. In the plan of God, Jesus is the focal point. All God's hopes and purposes for man and the world and the whole universe are summed up in Jesus Christ. Everything is ours in Jesus Christ, and anything good we have is only because of Jesus Christ. Brothers and sisters, *Up With the Son!*

15 « Joe Aldrich

Joe Aldrich is one of the three pastors at Mariners, the other two focusing their ministries on counseling and youth. Leaving seminary in 1971 after finishing a doctoral program, Joe came into the church, which had a climate and commitments already established through the leadership of the board. He soon fit in as a member of the team, for Joe's own vision and commitments paralleled those of the church. The striking growth of the congregation, from 250 to over 750 in two years, is certainly related to his coming. But just as certain is the fact that the foundation for growth was laid during the eight years of solid ministry before he came.

Joe's preaching ministry is essentially personal and practical. He has preached on topics that deal with the needs of the church as a body, but his focus is on family and relational needs of individuals. In the board meetings the men together pore over teachings about the church: in the pulpit Joe shares God's truths as they relate to opening up our lives to experience and express His beauty. This sermon gives the rich flavor of Joe's distinctive ministry of the Word.

Believers Make Better Lovers

Love is something that concerns all of us. In noticing some of the bumper stickers around lately, it's interesting to see the kinds of messages they convey. I saw one that says, "Milk drinkers make better lovers." I was raised on a farm and used to milk cows every morning and drink milk by the gallon, and it didn't help me a bit. And then you've probably seen this one:

"Dirty old men need love too." Now I don't think a dirty old man would know what love is, so I'm not sure about the truth of that. They probably need it, but they wouldn't recognize it if they saw it. The one I haven't been able to exegete or figure out says, "Goat ropers make better lovers." Now maybe some of you have an insight into that one, but somehow it got by me.

Huxley, a prolific writer, said that "of all the worn, smudged, dog-eared words in our vocabulary, love is surely the grubbiest, smelliest, slimiest, and yet it has to be pronounced, for after all, love is the last word." Well, it may be the last one, but it's a pretty slippery one, elusive, difficult to define. We say, "I love my wife, I love my baby, I love my biscuits dipped in gravy." *Love* has a broad spectrum of application! We've heard that love is "doing what comes naturally." Well, that isn't love; we don't naturally do what love really demands.

It's interesting to me that Paul's great concern as a bachelor was that people learn how to love, and he wrote in a letter to his friend Timothy, "Timothy, you're surrounded by men who are communicating a philosophy, and this philosophy of life will not produce love." It only leads to questions for which there is no answer — and endless discussion. In 1 Timothy 1, if you'll turn there, Paul tells Timothy there's only one provision in all the world that will set men free to be lovers. Here he's contrasting the teaching of the philosophers of the world, and the religious leaders of the world, with God's provision which he says is by faith. They have different objectives, and the fruit they produce are diametrically opposed. He's saying, "Timothy, you're surrounded by a philosophy of life that leads to futility. And it contradicts God's provision which is by faith."

Now, the word *provision* is one we run into in the Book of Ephesians. There this little word has been translated "dispensation," or "administration." It really means "household law." What is conveyed in this little term is the idea of *strategy*. Paul is saying that God has a strategy which can be worked out in human experiences, and this strategy is designed to make men free to love.

Notice that the next verse [1 Tim. 1:5] says, "But the goal of our instruction [in contradiction with the worldly philosophers] is love" which springs from three things: a pure heart, a clear conscience, and a sincere faith (NASB).

Paul goes on in the passage to develop a little more of the mental attitude of the worldly teachers, and in so doing he shows how they're wrong. He's basically saying these teachers involve men in *a competitive system of life.* "I compete with you" is really the Law principle. Now, competition and love cannot exist in the same household. If I'm competing with my mate or with my children or anyone else, there's no way I can love them. The two are mutually exclusive.

What Paul is saying is that God has a provision. This is the Good News — the gospel, which is designed to reach down into my life and confront the three greatest barriers to love. First, take the negative of these things, an impure heart — a defiled inner life. The second is guilt, or an unclear conscience. And the third is faith marked by hypocrisy or pretense.

It's interesting that Paul sets forth a sequence here that I think is significant to catch and keep in mind. He says first of all that when our lives are marked by impurity, impurity produces guilt. Impurity and guilt cannot be hidden from the world. People may not know the specifics of what we have done or how we have violated the basic principles of life, but violations cannot be hidden ultimately. Impurity produces guilt, and guilt produces pretense. We become fugitives — fugitives from the truth, fugitives from ourselves, and fugitives from other people, And Paul is also saying here that if a man is going to be set free to love, he has to deal with these three barriers, and there's not a genuine lover in the world who loves from an impure heart or an unclear conscience or a life marked by pretense.

The good news Paul is communicating to Timothy is, "Timothy, you don't have to be involved in a competitive system. God's provision, which is by faith, is designed to confront these barriers head-on." All I want to do this morning is to look at these three things, help you understand why this is so important, and trust that the Spirit of God will direct your gaze inward — but not leave it there. If we just look inward, it's discouraging. We have to look upward and see that God says, "That's okay; that's all right. I can understand that you have these problems in these areas of your life. But just don't claim to be innocent about it." That's the one great wall we erect between ourselves and God: it's only the wall — a claim to innocence.

Love

Now, Paul says that the goal of our instruction is love. Not to make us premillennial dispensationalists, or any other such things. The goal of all that we are doing — the Bible from cover to cover — is to make men and women who are lovers. When I think of love, two things come to mind, two purposes, two objectives.

Love involves, first of all, inviting someone else to walk at the head of the parade. That's what love is all about. We, when we do that which comes naturally, want to walk at the head of our parade. We want everyone else to admire us, and we want them all to be attendants. That isn't love. Love is giving that position to someone else and becoming an attendant in *their* parade. It's helping to focus the attention of others on them rather than on yourself. It's being excited about their growth and their development and their maturity, not your own.

That's pretty tough. We don't come by that naturally. I want to walk at the head of my parade, and I want everybody looking at me — that's natural. But if we really understand what Paul is saying, he's saying that *love* is a divine work. It's accomplished only through God's provision by faith, and it involves inviting someone else to march at the head of that parade.

I remember the disciples in the upper room. They weren't going to let anybody else march at the head of that parade. They wanted to be first, so they wouldn't wash each other's feet. Yet the real head of the parade — the Creator of the Universe — felt secure enough to wash their feet because He wasn't caught up in that competitive life style. He was secure in who He was.

The second thing about love is that it is designed to awaken beauty in the life of the other person. In other words, it focuses on that germinal beauty, that potential, which is there in another individual. Love's purpose is to provide a climate in which that beauty can blossom and grow.

I think a couple of words in Ephesians 5 can help us understand this process. The two words are *nourish* and *cherish*. I've mentioned these many times before, but I think it's appropriate to think again about how these words relate to the calling forth of beauty from someone else. Unfortunately, in human relationships we call forth an awful lot besides beauty. We call out a lot of ugliness, and that's because we're reacting with ugliness. A basic axiom of human response is that treatment determines temperament. If we're treated one way, that's how we respond.

Now that isn't the way it should be. The Bible principle is to return a blessing for an insult. This shuts down the process so that it doesn't escalate. But it isn't human nature. If you cross my path, look out! That's our inner attitude.

The word *nourish* means to provide all the nutriments for life, to provide all that is necessary for growth. In Ephesians 5, Paul in discussing the concept of love says that these are the two essential elements in communicating love. *Nourish* and *cherish*. So it's something for us to think about. What are we doing to provide nourishment for growth?

Many men might think, "Good night, I'm working hard fifty to sixty hours a week to bring home a paycheck. That's providing nourishment for growth." Well, many, many wives sitting in this room this morning would rather have their husbands take a massive cut in salary and commit themselves a little more to their homes and families. When the Bible talks about providing what is necessary for growth, the primary focus isn't on material things. It's providing that emotional affirmation and that spiritual affirmation that's so necessary for the development of beauty.

A personality is a function of relationship. If you don't like the personality of your wife or the personality of your husband, probably you're largely responsible for calling forth the negative qualities. If you respond in a negative way toward your husband all the time, those are the qualities in him that you will accentuate. You will bring them out, and they will become central in the relationship.

It's a negative feedback system. For example, the thermostat on the wall over here functions on the basis of a negative feedback system. It puts the machinery in motion only when it's either too hot or too cold. That's the way a lot of our personal relationships develop. We try to bring about change in that wife or that husband or that child only when he or she steps out of line! Then we're in there walloping, and it's negative. We're always trying to bring him from a negative to a positive.

These two words, *nourish* and *cherish,* tell us that God wants us to develop a positive feedback system where we're calling forth beauty rather than focusing on ugliness. You see, as long as we're in a competitive relationship, the negative is essential. We've got to come down hard on that ugliness because we haven't dealt with our own inner guilt and impurity; so we're always looking for the negative in the life of the other person, because that keeps the scale balanced.

Nourish — provide the nutriments for life and growth. Then Paul gets down to the root level with the second word, *cherish.* This focuses on an attitude. The word is used only one other time in the New Testament, in 1 Thessalonians 2, where it speaks of a woman holding a nursing child to her breast. The root of the verb is *to warm.* Talk about tenderness! As I was thinking about this, I thought of a rosebud. If I had a rosebud up here this morning, you would look at it and, because you know the potential of that rosebud, would know that even though it's beautiful as a bud, there is locked up inside it an even more incredible beauty.

The revelation of that beauty isn't automatic. Two things are required if that rosebud is going to open up and reveal inner beauty. The first is nourishment: It has to have the nutriments provided which are essential to life. Forget to water it, leave it in the pot, and just neglect it for four or five weeks and see what happens. Don't forget to feed it, to care about it, to check the insects that are chewing on it. But that isn't enough. The rosebud also needs the warmth of the sun. As it gets proper nourishment and the warmth of the sun to cherish, then it begins to open and reveal its inner beauty. And that's what love is designed to do: To call forth from the heart of the object of love a response of beauty which cannot be produced by will alone.

It's quite a task to be called to do that kind of thing. Paul says to Timothy, "Timothy, I want you to produce a crop of lovers there at Ephesus, and it's not going to be produced by getting caught up in a philosophy of life which is purely involved in speculation and questions for which there are no answers. It's discovered only through God's provision by faith, which is a provision designed to attack frontally the three barriers which hinder us from calling forth beauty in the life of another person."

The three barriers

What are these three barriers? I'm putting these in a negative sense, for it's clear that if love comes from a pure heart, this love must be blocked by an impure heart. So I'm going to be looking at these barriers from a negative perspective. Impurity of heart. In Proverbs 4:23 it says, "Keep thy heart with all diligence; for out of it are the issues of life." Keep it with all diligence. In other words, guard it as your most precious possession because as a man's heart is, so his life is. Impurity there is going to be reflected in impurity of relationship.

You have probably seen that little booklet, *My Heart Christ's Home.* It suggests that if Jesus Christ is in your home, what room in the home have you got Him trapped in? You know, "Hey, Lord, sit in the parlor — we've got the mantel dusted and the proper magazines scattered around here." And suppose He gets up and checks on a few things first, "And you run in, and you stick a few things under the couch, and shout, 'Now come on in, Lord . . .'" What about the attic? Would Christ feel comfortable in the attic of your life? Or the basement?

God wants us to be walking in the light. That means having a mental attitude by which we invite the searching gaze of the Holy God to penetrate to the very depths of our being and reveal what's there, and that's the only way not to be a fugitive. When Cain confronted the Lord, the Lord could handle murder. But Cain said, "No, I'm not my brother's keeper!" He claimed innocence and continued to erect that wall. Our attitude has to be the attitude of David who said, "Search me, O God, and know my heart; . . . and see if there be any wicked way in me, and lead me in the way everlasting" [Ps. 139:23, 24].

I think the sequence here is very important in dealing with the root problem — the problem of a defiled inner life, which produces guilt. We always have the problem, and it produces guilt, and guilt produces pretense — a life of hypocrisy. All of these kill any chances of love's being expressed. If your heart is impure, and God's love is trying to be expressed through that, it's going to be contaminated. If your conscience is laden with guilt, and God's love is trying to be expressed through that, it's going to be confined. If your life is marked by hypocrisy or pretense, and God's love is trying to be expressed through you, it'll be counterfeit, and the world will reject the Savior because of the kind of love that they see coming through your life.

So Paul is saying that at the root love springs from a pure heart. It's interesting that the word *pure* doesn't mean "pure from the beginning." It is actually the Greek word *katharidzo,* from which we get the word *catharsis.* It's a "cleaned" or a "purged" heart. This gives us hope, because every one of us has blown the blueprint, and our hearts are or have been marked at times by the impure.

Now, aren't you thankful it doesn't say "inadequate hearts," because we're all inadequate. But God has made provision for the impure. The Word says that "if we walk in the light, as He is in the light; we have fellowship one with another, and the blood of Jesus Christ His Son [keeps on cleansing] us from all unrighteousness."

More important than *how* you walk is *where* you walk. You see, a man who has impurity in his life and will not deal with it has to flee the light. If we could go to those who have been condemned to hell for eternity and ask them if they would like to come into heaven, 100 percent of them would say no for one reason: They couldn't stand the penetrating gaze of absolute holiness.

The only way that you and I will ever stand in the presence of God is by His provision by faith of the righteousness of Christ being put to our account. That's why Jude gets so excited in the last verse of his epistle when he says, "Now unto him that is able to keep you from falling, and to present you faultless . . ." [v. 24 KJV]. *We've got to deal with purity of life, and this isn't an act — this is a process!* There has to be a mental attitude that we carry with us throughout our lives, that by God's grace I'm committed to maintaining inner purity and integrity. And if I'm not committed to that, I'm going to destroy myself and destroy my family and I'm going to become more and more alienated from those I love.

Believe me, the people whom I see week after week in counseling sessions show that the violation usually begins at this point — they haven't dealt with the problem of inner purity. They're continually fugitives. What a horrible price to pay! It reminds me of the passage in Proverbs that occurs three or four times — "a way which seems right to a man, but its end is the way of death" [cf. 14:12 rsv]. Death — being not only an event that we all face someday, but a process of disintegration and decay of seeking for goals that are not legitimate goals, and in the process destroying the most significant gifts that God has given — those relationships. It involves the husband and wife, the father and son, the mother and daughter.

Paul says, "Timothy, you've got to teach your people that if they want to be lovers, it has to begin with a pure heart." And I trust that you will allow the Spirit of God to run around in your own life a little bit and that your desire will be the desire of David: "Search me, O God, and know my heart; . . . and see if there be any wicked way in me, and lead me into the way everlasting." If that's your desire, then you have the right mental attitude to begin to deal with the second problem — the problem of guilt.

Guilt is the product of violation. We can deal with impurity, and experience release from guilt in our relationships with God, but we've still wronged a lot of people in the process. The second barrier Paul mentions is the whole area of conscience. Someone has defined a conscience as "the thing in me that feels bad when everything else feels good." I think that's a pretty good definition of conscience, but I actually think of conscience as God's moral inlay — it's a compass He's put inside me which is directing me to the fact that there's moral law in this universe.

Every man has a conscience. The problem is that often our conscience has become seared. Timothy is told that people can have a cauterized conscience. We know that as children we are often innocent and have a very sensitive conscience. But something happens as we grow up. We don't go running back and asking forgiveness and saying that we're sorry for these dinky little things, the way we used to when we were children. A man can become so cauterized and insensitive that the voice of conscience is virtually dead. And that's tragic, because it destroys a built-in compass that is to direct him back to the fact that God has established laws and principles in this universe; if we violate them, we hurt ourselves. The conscience is designed to tell me that my heart's impure.

Now, if my heart is impure, you can't see my conscience, but you can see my pretense! You don't have to be around a person very long to see whether he's a phony. Let's face it, all of us have areas of our lives in which we're not walking in relationship to what we know.

Our consciences are constantly seeking to be alleviated of guilt. You know if we have guilt we want to get rid of it. A letter came to the IRS from a conscience-stricken taxpayer, and the letter said, "My conscience bothered me and here's $170 which I owe in back taxes." And there was a little P.S. at the bottom of the letter: "If my conscience still bothers me, I'll send in the rest."

You know, man will do anything to get off the hook of his conscience. One way is by rationalization. "Everybody else is doing it," so a person begins to accept a statistical morality rather than a biblical morality. But if he has any inkling of God's truth, he can't get away with it. It stays there, and he begins to use more and more and more psychic energy repressing this guilt. Bishop Gore said, "Man's first duty is not to follow his conscience but to enlighten it." So if you're really committed to purity of heart, something's going to happen, because you're going to be in the Word, you're going to be growing, you're going to be developing, you're going to be restructuring that conscience, and to do that you're going to be forced to deal with guilt. You cannot ignore it any longer.

One of the products of guilt is self-punishment. A woman was guilty of adultery in her marriage, and her husband didn't know it. She kept it a secret for ten years, and it literally consumed her. So she thought that to alleviate this guilt she'd tell her husband, and it would solve the problem. She told her husband, but it didn't solve the problem, and one day her husband came home to see her with a child that she loved dearly. She was choking the child to death — punishing herself in this way, trying to find release from that guilt.

Many of us live a life style of self-punishment for two reasons. First, we don't believe there's now "no condemnation" from God's standpoint to those who are in Christ Jesus. And second, we're not willing to go to whomever we have wronged and make it right. Scripture says we need to acknowledge guilt, not only before God, but also before men. Remember the prodigal son: When he came home he said two things to his father. He said, "Father, I've sinned against heaven. I'm acknowledging the fact that I have had an impure life before God." And, "I've sinned against you." You see, he dealt with the total dimension of his wrong.

Often we just want to deal with the vertical, and say, "God, you know I've sinned against you." But that doesn't deal with guilt. I know that in my own life there were some areas in which whenever I thought I'd get right with God, these things kept cropping up; I'd keep saying, "Lord, forgive me for this," and I'd keep telling myself, "Well, Lord, I know that you've forgiven me." But for some reason my conscience continued to condemn me. Finally I had to go to a professor and tell him that I'd cheated on some exams, and I had to go to a gal whom I had wronged and say, "Will you forgive me?" I had to go to an employer and set some things right, and then I was set free.

A notable passage in Matthew 5 says that if you're presenting your offering at the altar and remember that your brother has something against you, leave your offering there before the altar and go your way and be reconciled to your brother. Then come and present your gift. I almost think God is seeing a compensation-type response. He sees someone who senses a tremendous need to give a gift, and Christ, being aware of human nature, says, "Look, why are you bringing this gift? Are you compensating? Trying to ease your conscience, feeling that if you make a sacrificial gift, somehow you can get out of being reconciled to your brother? Or that somehow if you get involved in all kinds of Christian activity, and supporting people, and cleaning the church, God will let you off the hook and won't force you to go back and make right those wrongs?

"No," Christ says. "Forget the gift — it's really not important whether you give it at all. Go back to that brother who has been wronged and be reconciled."

Paul says we're sent out into life armed with two things: faith — that's the ability to reach out and to believe and grasp and lay hold of God's provisions — and second, a clear conscience. Now if we're missing either one or both of these we're not really equipped for battle. There must be faith in an absolutely sovereign God, who has joined you to Himself, joined you to One who knows no failure, but who is adequate in every way. But you can't function unless there's a clear conscience. This has to be a continuing attitude toward life.

The last thing Paul mentions is a life without pretense. The word *sincere* means literally "not to speak from under a mask." I think this is what the world sees. This is why the world rejects Christ. The number one complaint of the man out there who is not attending a church somewhere or joined to a body of believers is that "they're hypocrites." And Christ condemns such pretense. He says, "Beware of practicing your righteousness before men to be noticed by them. . . . When you pray, you are not to be as the hypocrites; for they love to stand and pray in synagogues and on street corners, in order to be seen by men. . . . Whenever you fast, do not put on a gloomy face as the hypocrites do; for they neglect their appearance in order to be seen fasting by men" [Matt. 6:1, 5, 16 NASB].

I think many of us are like Freddie the Frog. Freddie the Frog fell in a rut, and his friends came by and they looked down and they said, "Hey, Freddie, what are you doing in the rut?" And he answered, "I fell in and I can't get out. I've been trying hard, but it's hopeless." So his friends offered their condolences and went on their way, and they came back a little later and were surprised to discover that Freddie was out of the rut. So they went looking for him and found him hopping around in the grass, as frogs do, and they said, "Hey, it's great to see you, Freddie! Thought you were stuck in an impossible rut." "I was," he said, "but a big Mack truck came along, and I had to get out."

Sometimes God has to run a big Mack truck right through the middle of our lives to help us to understand that. Look, if you're going to be set free to be a lover, it's not going to be an easy process. You have some basic, root areas of your life that you've got to deal with. Otherwise you're not going to have the freedom that's so necessary to life.

As you reflect on some of your inabilities to love as God wants you to, remember that these are the three basic barriers that have to come down. An impure heart, an unclear conscience, and a life marked by pretense. I trust you'll allow the Spirit of God to minister to your own hearts in whatever area of need He feels necessary.

16 « Gib Martin

Gib finds it difficult to view himself as a preacher. He tells of the early years of ministry when he noticed he was losing his audience when he spoke. He faced this head-on, poring over books on preaching from all the historical and modern traditions of every denomination. And out of his study and experience he developed his own preaching style.

But when asked for a tape, Gib sent a cassette of the opening session of one of his Sunday evening "schools of Christian living." In this tape, edited down from two hours, Gib shares, with eighty or more enrollees, principles of counseling.

The tape is characteristic of Gib's ministry. It reflects his total confidence that God the Holy Spirit can and will equip the believer-priest to *serve*. It reflects a commitment to Scripture and the willingness to build *everything* in his life on God's revelation that marks the believer who has come to know how trustworthy God really is. And it reflects the compassion and acceptance with which Gib and the men and women of Trinity touch others' lives. You and I gain a deep insight into the character of the pastoral ministry at Trinity by sitting in now as Gib launches into counseling by teaching "The Christian *Can* Counsel."

The Christian Can Counsel

When Henry David Thoreau was nine years old, someone asked him what he would be when he grew up. He answered, "Probably I'll be myself." And he was, too, one of the most

independent minds of his time. An article in *Sunshine* maga-
zine comments, "How many of us in the adult world can say
we are ourselves?" Instead our identities are submerged in our
jobs, our social positions, our functions as parents, as voters and
homeowners.

To be one's self does not mean to run wild, to ignore obliga-
tions, to rebel for its own sake (as adolescents sometimes seem
to think). It means rather to see one's self first and foremost as
a person, not as a part of a person, not as an American, not as
a male or female, but as a living organism composed of body
and soul and spirit. Most of us live locked tightly in our partial
little loyalties and thus never realize the fullness of being a person. We approach the world sideways like a crab, seeing it only
from the oblique angle of our particular social status, our background, our special vocation.

But to be distinctively human means to share with God a
panoramic view of the world, including one's self. It means
rising above the accidental prison of our personalities to discover what human beings really should be like. This is a difficult task, but it is the only worthwhile one in life. Compared to
it, making money is frivolous, and having fun is dull.

The Bible is a unique book when it comes to discovering what
human beings are and what they can be. Its teachings have
been tested in the laboratory of human history. When it speaks
about man's nature, about man's behavior, about man's attitudes
and what motivates man, it is the most relevant source known
to us. All the books written in the world cannot improve on the
written Word of God. This is one reason why it is important
to look at counseling from a biblical, theistic perspective.

Finding freedom: prerequisite to counseling

Isaiah, speaking prophetically, said of Christ, "His name will
be called 'Wonderful Counselor, Mighty God, Everlasting Father, Prince of Peace'" [9:6]. The reason why Jesus was and
is the best counselor known to man is that He was true to Himself, to His unique being. He lived under the authority of God
the Father, and He was forthright with all men regardless of
the status of their lives, be it low and humble, be it high and
elevated.

He looked at men in terms of their hearts, not in terms of their status or class. He did not participate in any of the games people play. He proclaimed, "You will know the truth, and the truth will make you free" [John 8:32]. It was a simple message, it was a dynamic message, it is a message that still stirs the hearts of those who hear it, if they really hear those words.

This week a friend was talking with me, and I mentioned something about truth setting people free. His eyes got big, and he said, "Would you say that again? It's beautiful!" I said, "Well, that's what Jesus says," and he was excited; it was almost like a new thought. All of a sudden it struck a note in his mind and gave him a new idea, a new hope.

"The truth will make you free," Jesus said. Every human heart cries, utterly cries, to be free. There is not one of you who sometime in your life has not cried to be free. I trust that everyone here tonight *is* free. But there's no human heart that doesn't cry to be free, free of the awful self that keeps tormenting us, destroying us, dragging us down, and perverting us. This freedom is offered to all men by the greatest counselor known to humankind, by Jesus Christ Himself.

With Jesus Christ as our great and flawless example, we can readily see that counseling begins with a life well lived, and not in theory well taught. This truth is fundamental to becoming a counselor guided by the loving Holy Spirit. The world refuses to adopt this principle, but that does not give the church the same privilege. Jesus reminds us in the Sermon on the Mount, "You, therefore, must be perfect [mature]" [Matt. 5:48].

In that context, Matthew 5, the stress is on God's goodness to all. We're told He is good to the just and the unjust. He is consistent with Himself; He is good. And a Christian counselor to be truly effective must also be good; he must be consistent with himself. Remember, God never exhorts us to be what we cannot be. For one day, one hour, one moment of time, the child of God can be mature in his walk with God and before men. This is the standard set before us. This is the standard I believe every counselor ought to set for himself or herself in this ministry.

Now, according to this principle, the most important matter in a counseling encounter is the life of the counselor. Too often we dwell on the life of the counselee. But if the one being sought out to counsel is immature in his or her life style, then the counselee is in great danger of receiving and believing spurious guidance.

Commitment to truth. Keep this in mind always: Only the truth will set men free. You have not helped anyone at all by giving him something that is not the truth. No matter how clever you might think it is, or how you might manipulate the situation so you look good in it, it doesn't help. What I'm saying is that we are to bring men to the truth. To be a counselor, you must recognize that fact and live with it realistically.

Remember that it is not the counselor's technique or his knowledge of psychological terminology that is important. God looks upon the heart of man. He examines the spirit, to see first of all if we are honest with what we are handling, if we are loving in our attitude, and if we are pure in heart. It is this kind of person you can trust to counsel. A truly mature person will possess these characteristics, and people will seek them out for counsel. They will see the truth in their lives.

Counseling defined. This commitment of the believer to truth helps us come to a definition of counseling. The definition really isn't very scientific, it isn't profound, and it probably would not fit into any of the books by psychiatrists that you might read. I'll put it this way: "Counseling is the ministry of service by which a person helps another solve a hassle, a hangup, or a conflict *with the sole purpose of helping that person on to maturity!*"

Counseling can be done individually or in group situations. We have a lot of group counseling. We don't sit down and analyze it as groups counseling, but I do it every day in some way. And it's beautiful . . . it's such a beautiful thing to see many people bring counsel in a gentle way to a person. Counsel that confirms truth and helps a person to take ahold of it and start moving.

Counseling extends freedom. Under Christian counseling, the counselee must be absolutely free to reject the counsel given, without feeling guilty or condemned. I shared this with a man the other day, and he said, "That's not true in our church." But it's true in the Bible. And it needs to be true when we're talking to a person. We evaluate him. We judge him, condemn him, or look down at him — not lift him up, make him feel more human, more accepted.

A great part of the healing process is wrapped up in man's need to be free. Freedom is a gift from God; therefore we must exhibit this gift in our lives. If I have to make people feel guilty or condemned for not following the counsel I give, I'm not free. And the world needs examples of men and women who are free inside and out. One example of freedom in the life of a person is better than many books on the subject . . . and we are to be that example.

Faith's content: key to competency

Working under the definition I've given, you can realize that every believer whose faith has content potentially can counsel.

If I could bring one of you up here (and I might one of these nights), I'd say, "Tell everyone here how to receive Jesus Christ as Savior and Lord. You have about eighty seconds." What would you say? How would you nail that down? Now that's content . . . being able to express and explain truth. Later we'll look at some case studies. You'll see how to approach particular situations and what kind of answers you can provide. Having content is being able to express a Christian world view, Bible truth. Having content is also tied to maturity: we realize our full potential as a servant of the living God by understanding and living truth. Such a person is a qualified counselor in the sight of God. Regardless of what behavorial science may say, that person is qualified to give counsel. Such a person is able to help another person solve a conflict in his life.

I said this to someone one day, and he said, "Well, you could never help a nuclear physicist with his problems." And I said, "I beg to differ with you." I would never try to help a nuclear physicist solve his problems in nuclear physics. If he had a problem in nuclear physics and was dumb enough to come to me, I would seek out someone to help him. But for the truly competent Christian who has faith's content well together, there is no one in this world whom he can't help in some way.

I remember eleven years ago the head of the psychology department of the University of Florida, about sixty-four years old then, came to a Bible class I was teaching in Tallahassee. I was scared to death. When he walked into that class, I whispered to Linda, "Pray that he'll leave." I felt absolutely, completely discombobulated by his presence, for I'd heard he was coming to examine this young character who was teaching the Word. Well, he didn't leave. He sat there as if he were drinking in everything that I said. I said to myself, he can't be doing that. When I finished, the professor came to me and said, "I've never heard these things. Where have I been?"

Now, I really wasn't qualified to help the head of the psychology department at the University of Florida in terms of psychology. But I was able to help him solve the greatest hassle that he had in his life, that of getting to know Jesus Christ. That night we spent about five hours together, and he bowed his knee to Jesus. It was a marvelous experience, one of the highlights of my life while I was in Tallahassee. He was always coming over to my house to get fed. He'd have a few minutes between classes, and he'd run over to see if I was home, because He was so hungry inside.

We can help *anyone* if we've got our faith together. Everybody needs what we have when it comes to Jesus. Everyone needs love, and everybody needs compassion. Everyone needs to feel someone is concerned about him. Many times when these basic needs are satisfied, they can solve their own problems. Hassles are not nearly so big as the person thought they were. That's why I don't think I'm a very good counselor. I have a lot of people come to me, but I don't really offer them much counsel. I just sit around loving them. I try to understand them. I believe in them, and they solve their own problems.

Biblical principles from James

"By his good life let him show his works in the meekness of wisdom. But if you have bitter jealousy and selfish ambition in your hearts, do not boast and be false to the truth. This wisdom is not such that comes down from above, but is earthly, unspiritual, devilish. For where jealousy and selfish ambition exist, there will be disorder and every vile practice. But the wisdom from above is first pure, then peaceable, gentle, open to reason, full of mercy and good fruits, without uncertainty or insincerity. And the harvest of righteousness is sown in peace by those who make peace" [3:13-18].

A good life. First, James points out that counseling begins

with a life well lived: "By his good life let him show his works."
He then points out that there is a wisdom not from God; it's
earthly, sensual, impure. Finally he defines the nature of divine
wisdom and understanding.

Let's look at this sequence. James says in verse 17, "It is first
pure." That is, God's wisdom is unpolluted. Here is the reason
why we need to experience reality before we give counsel. What
we give to another should have the clear ring of divine authority. Jesus, our Example, spoke as one who has authority.
The apostles in the early church spoke with authority. They
were untrained men, but they spoke as having authority.

The apostle Peter writes, "As each has received a gift, em-
ploy it for one another, as good stewards of God's varied grace:
whoever speaks [and we can translate this word *gives counsel*]
as one who utters oracles of God" [1 Peter 4:10, 11]. In other
words, we are to speak out of the authority of the Word of God,
which we ourselves experience.

A peaceable spirit. Second, wisdom is peaceable. God's wisdom, when applied by the counselee, will produce a peaceable
spirit in that person. Thus a truly effective counselor needs to
demonstrate a peaceable spirit. Peace helps a person to focus on
Jesus, and not upon you. If the counselee starts worrying about
you because you have no peace, and you're a bit frantic with
him, he focuses on the wrong person. The focus is to be on the
One who is there to deliver him from bondage. Peace is a mani-
festation of His presence. If there is no peace in your life, there
is no presence. Peace gives the counselee a sense of confidence
in the counselor.

I can remember when I used to sit down in the basement
in my office and people were going to come in and counsel with
me, and I had them on my schedule. I'd think, *What am I going to say?* And God wouldn't give me answers. Heaven was
closed. I'd start reading, searching, but that was good because
I got to read the Bible that way anyhow. At least I read the
Bible, and God was planting seeds and thoughts. But when
people came in, I'd have nothing to say, and I couldn't understand that. I was anxious. The Scriptures say, "Don't be
anxious" — and I read that, yet I was. And so I went through
this traumatic experience of always being anxious.

One day I said, "Lord, I'll never be anxious again when any-

one walks in that door. By faith I'll choose not to be anxious."
You know what? I'm not anxious any more! Faith liberates us
to obey. And when I quit being anxious, people suddenly said,
"Well, at least he's not anxious. He doesn't know much, but
at least he's not anxious," and they felt more confident too.

You can see why James said wisdom from above is peaceable.
How important it is that you're at peace listening, and you're
at peace with what you say, or even with what you don't say.

Now, to maintain a peaceable spirit is a difficult thing. It is
a moment-by-moment process many times. Pressures will come.
But peace we must seek from God. Peace will be perceived in
your voice, it will be perceived in your attitude. So keep in
mind that wisdom from above is peaceable always.

A gentle approach. The divine wisdom is gentle. This also
means it's forbearing. This concept points us to the kindness
of our great God. All counsel should glorify God and in a sense
reflect His attribute. The things we say in some way should
portray the attribute of the One on whose behalf we are speaking. All counsel, then, should glorify Him. Truly God has been
gentle with us. When I think of His gentleness with me, I want
to weep. Think about it tonight: He is gentle with us, and this
is the pattern to follow in our counsel.

It is important to note that gentleness is a fruit of the Holy
Spirit. This brings us back to the thesis that the foremost task
of the counselor is to learn how to be counseled in his or her
own life by the Holy Spirit while he or she is giving counsel.
I cannot possibly be gentle if I'm not listening for the Holy
Spirit's encouragement. Some things people say to me make me
angry, and I have to restrain myself. I know I will not help
them, and I'll give myself ulcers as well. So gentleness is a fruit
of the Holy Spirit.

Paul told young Timothy, "The Lord's servant must not be
quarrelsome but kindly to every one" [2 Tim. 2:24]. How
many? To everyone. You know, it's easy to be gentle with the
nice people, but what about those characters you have to deal
with? Paul continues, "Forbearing, correcting his opponents
with gentleness."

Wisdom from above is gentle. I have in my notes the statement, "Test all counsel by this unique factor." If you are not
being gentle, then I'm not sure you are really in the Spirit.

There's much counseling that I have done when I was not gentle; I did not see much fruit from it. I have learned since then to test my counseling by this principle.

Openness. Next, God's wisdom is open to reason. In simple language, the person seeking counsel will feel free to express himself or herself in words, in tears, in feelings, in utter desperation, in four-letter words, in cursing, or in anger. This is why the person has sought you out. He feels that he can ventilate, pour out, his heart and still somehow be considered a person when he's through. He is looking for someone who will make sense out of what appears to be a total mess. He is looking for a positive solution to his negative experience. So we must be easy to approach. We must understand his state of mind. We must be open to his kind of reason.

This concept teaches us to be slow to speak, not to rebuke for wrong things.

I used to rebuke people for swearing in my office, and I lost control of the counseling situation every time. I never got to the root of their problem. But I didn't like people swearing in my office. What was I going to do about that? It was as if one day God said, "That's tough." And when I heard that, it came through. I said, "Okay, I'll get tough." I just let it happen. It only happens once or twice with a counselee. If people can really get it out, and you can cover that with love — maybe it's the first time anyone has covered their sin with love — then they become more reasonable. This kind of foul language quickly passes away, and they can talk a normal way. We must not rebuke for the wrong thing.

We must pray for the one who is sharing, seeking some light to guide him out of the confusion and darkness he's in. So the wisdom of God is open to reason — the counselee's kind of reason. The life of our Lord proves that fully. He did not rebuke people needing counsel. He went to the root cause and provided healing. He was able to bend without breaking, to yield without compromising.

James then says, "Wisdom from above is . . . full of mercy." Far too often, those who give counsel lack fullness of mercy. To lack in mercy is to be without compassion for another human being. Jesus taught, "Blessed are the merciful, for they shall obtain mercy." Mercy, biblically, is the mingling of righteousness with godly love. Mercy allows us to cover sin until we discern the root cause of attitudes, behaviors, and deeds or misdeeds. It doesn't say we retreat from righteousness. It's the mingling of righteousness and love in a propitious way, so that we can listen and follow the careful guidance of the Holy Spirit in a given situation.

The simple reason why we often fail to be full of mercy is that we fail to see the pit from which we ourselves have been drawn. When I see haughty Christians, I know they have never yet faced up to Jeremiah 17:9, 10. They still have a very shallow, weak concept of their own sinfulness. They do not see themselves as being as vile and awful as they really are . . . and yet as cherished by God as we can be.

So we need to understand grace. To be truly competent in our counsel, we need to understand grace sufficiently to share it without expectation of any return on our investment. That'll give a few of you hangups. We think we are always entitled to returns on our investments! No, you don't — not if you're going to be a counselor from God's perspective. There are no immediate returns on spiritual investments of your money or your time. Jesus has been waiting centuries for His investment to pay off. And some of us have a hard time waiting ten minutes on a fellow man! It's a serious rebuke to us. But the church still has the answer, praise God!

We can be the kind of counselors God intended us to be, and we can take to the world this kind of message. It's dynamic! It sets men free, and I love it. The more I walk with Jesus, the more I love Him; and the more I walk in His truth, the more I love it, because I realize how true it is.

Frequently people say, "I can't believe it, Gib." I say, "Don't worry about it. I can." They say, "Well, that's not going to help me!" But it will. Paul said, "Let me be your example." A counselor literally feeds the one he is serving the good fruit of his or her own life. Understanding how that good fruit became a part of your life style will be a great asset in your counseling ministry.

How did freedom happen in your life? Start thinking about what you've experienced and begin putting it together so that you can share it with someone else. That's what Christianity is supposed to do: to pass love and truth along. Too often we pass our experiences along, and people say, "Oh, they had a wonderful experience." It becomes a boasting thing. We're not supposed to be always passing our experiences along. It's wonderful to pass one along occasionally as an illustration, but let's also pass *truth* along. Understand how you arrived at the truth, then pass that along, and then you will be strengthening your brother.

Honesty with all. James says, finally, God's wisdom is without partiality, uncertainty, or hypocrisy. This means we are to be sincere, without guile. I want to make one brief statement about sincerity. It is one of the most evasive concepts in the English language. Many people are dead sincere, but they are dead wrong. People often say, "I was really sincere, Gib." That's not the kind of sincerity James is talking about. It is the sincerity that comes out of a right relationship, a right concept of life, and it's without guile. It doesn't mean we know everything, but it means what we know, we know well, and we can pass it along as testable.

It also means that the Christian counselor does not treat the rich better than the poor, or vice versa. No partiality. I know those who condemn the rich and are smug in that attitude. That's not of God either.

When people come for counsel, they think I'm serving them, but I'm really not. I'm serving God so they can be better servants of His when they leave me. Yes, I provide a service to them, but I'm serving Him, and therefore there's a sense of certainty in what I say and do. If I keep my mind in contact with His mind, then what I say to them will not sway them, even though it might not drive them to the truth in terms of their problems. At least it won't hurt them.

It's rather like neurotics who go to doctors and get sugar-coated pills occasionally. The doctor knows they simply need to swallow something. This means that not everything I give or you give to a person is going to help him solve his problem, but it certainly is not going to hinder the solving of it, if we have that sense of certainty of whom we are serving and the source of our information.

A wise counselor will be aware of his or her own weaknesses and thus will never attempt to cover, or manipulate, in order to make people think he is more wise than he really is. God's wisdom is without hypocrisy. We must refrain from hypocrisy.

And hypocrisy is covering, not letting people know what we don't know.

Counseling, then, begins with a life well lived, and not simply theory well taught. Technique is important. But our life style is decisive. Keep that in mind: It's the most important thing I've said tonight. Our life style is decisive. People need an example of the truth in living form. In Christ we can and should give the world that much-needed example. As counselors we *must* be an example if our counseling is to carry out man's most important mission — to glorify God.